Some thoughts on prayer from Louis Evely:

You do not have to "look for" God. If you do, you will never find him, because he is never anywhere other than where you are.

Prayer is listening to God's prayer to us.

God speaks in his Word, but also in our life.

Prayer is offering ourselves to God so that he may have a chance of doing in us what he is always wanting to do, but is prevented from doing by our going away before he has had a chance to begin.

Prayer is not asking things of God but receiving what he wants to give you.

To be able to receive a gift you have to know how to open yourself.

There is nothing more pharisaical than wanting to be worthy of God's love before understanding that he loves us unworthy.

Praying is reminding ourselves of God's plan for the salvation of the world and his appeal for our collaboration in it.

God is in you, as he is in every creature; waiting to be guessed at, prayed to, listened to, so that he can grow in you.

LOUIS EVELY

OUR PRAYER

IMAGE BOOKS

A DIVISION OF DOUBLEDAY & COMPANY, INC.

GARDEN CITY, NEW YORK

Image Books edition by special arrangement with
Seabury Press
Image Books edition published September 1974

Original edition: *La Prière d'un Homme Moderne,*
Paris, Editions de Seuil, 1969.
Translated by Paul Burns.

CONTENTS

Our Prayer

INTRODUCTION

Come Holy Spirit

The heading itself is an example of reality being the opposite of what we think. It is not we who call the Holy Spirit, but he who calls us. Let us not reverse our roles any longer.

We only invoke because we have been convoked; we only aspire because we have been inspired. Our appeals do not decide God's gifts; they only measure them. Our loftiest ambitions are never any more than consent to his plans. God bestows on us far more than we can ever accept from him.

There is nothing more pagan than the adage: "Man proposes and God disposes." This would make man God's toy, and God no more than a capricious despot. What actually happens is that God proposes and man disposes. God is pure proposal, calling, grace: "Behold, I stand at the door and knock; if anyone hears my voice and opens the door, I will come in to him and eat with him, and he with me" (Rev. 3, 20). God proposes himself and we dispose of him.

This is the best news I can give you: you are not alone; you are not hunting in the dark. God is calling you; he wants you far more than you want him; he is far more anxious to meet you than you are to meet him. Without him, you would not even be starting out on the way: "No one can come to me, unless my Father draw him . . ." Because if you were to look for him by yourself, what assur-

ance would you have of finding him? But when he looks for
you, you cannot miss him.

The only difference between the saints and us (and it is
much less than you think) is that they are careful to wel
come and remind themselves of the impressions that God
makes on them. Do not think that God loved the saints more
than you, that he favored them with exceptional graces,
chose them as his "privileged few." No, God is just as in
tent on each of us, his ambition for us is boundless, his pro
posal equally generous to each of us; it is only our response
that differs. God loves us all equally, as much as we allow
ourselves to be loved, as far as we open ourselves to his love
He beckons everyone, but forces no one.

Christ said: "If your brother offends you, rebuke him in
private; if he listens to you, you will have regained your
brother. If he does not listen to you, take one or two more
people with you . . . if he does not listen to them tell it to
the Church (which is precisely a group of people who love
one another); if he does not listen to the Church either,
hold him as you would a pagan or a publican"—which does
not mean "as someone you do not love," since you are
bound to love even your enemies, but as someone with
whom you are unable to establish those close ties of recipro
cal intimacy that depend on mutual consent.

So God's love for us is proportioned to our response, per
fectly adjusted to each individual, though not arbitrarily.
God wants to enter into the most lively and affectionate re
lationship possible with each one of us; he is limited only
by our refusal. The limit to our sanctification is not God's
lack of generosity, but our resistance to it: "It is not by
measure that he gives the Spirit" (John 3, 34). The angels
of the Annunciation, of Gethsemani and the Resurrection
hover continually over the sons and daughters of our age,
but rarely find a place upon which to set down.

To be able to receive a gift you have to know how to
open yourself. But when a person is making the gift of him-

self, then it is very hard—for to receive him you must give yourself. You cannot possess a person; you cannot count a person among your goods. To receive someone who is giving himself to you, you have to give yourself to him just as fully, just as earnestly as you want him.

You do not even have to "look for" God. If you do, you will never find him, because he is never anywhere other than where you are. All your efforts to chase him merely take you away from him. You don't have to find him, just accept the offer of himself that he has always been making. You do not need to go and meet him, just let him come and meet you.

In prayer, we realize that God came to meet us a long time ago: "So long I have been with you, Philip, and you have not yet recognized me?"

Prayer is listening to God's prayer to us. The truth and the difficulty of prayer are to be found in this fact; prayer is not man's idea, not his ambition, illusion or auto-suggestion. It is making oneself available to the total truth of one's life.

The person who does not pray becomes self-sufficient, closed in on himself, withdrawn into himself. The person who does pray believes that there is more in our universe than he has already seen, and he watches for signs that might be addressed to him, but as anxious not to invent them as not to miss them. Christ tells us that he who looks will find, who asks will receive, who knocks will have the door opened to him. But the person who prays is liable to find that he was found a long time ago, that he has already received what he is asking for, that the door has been opened before he has time to knock, and that he has always been listened to. This is what the disciples discovered at the Resurrection.

Mary Magdalen was lost and distracted; she threw herself into a search for him, but it was he who was looking for her. He called her, saying her name in the way that only he could, and she found herself again in finding him in the place she was trying to escape from. A name is a call, a vocation; it takes time to learn to love one's name, to recognize yourself in its sound. It all depends on the voice that says it, but what joy there is in being able to recognize yourself in your name, to accept yourself in the voice that calls you.

The disciples on the road to Emmaus thought their search was over and they were right to go away. But he interrupted them and dragged them out of their gloomy reflections, gently soothing them by talking to them about themselves and himself in the way that only he could, and then leading them into the celebration of a real Eucharist. Brought back to their calling, they went away knowing that it was not he who had left them, but they who had left him.

The apostles on Lake Tiberias were agonizing over their setback and his absence. But he renewed his call to them, and made them relive the wonder of their calling. He showed them that it could all begin again, even better than before. While they thought they were alone, he was preparing this feast for them, and they learned that he would never abandon them, however lost they might get. They learned, as we should learn, that meeting God is not a chance happening, nor something we can merit or win, but faithful companionship, a tender call, a humble appeal from him, and that what was extraordinary about their lives was not that God appeared amongst them, but that, for once, they recognized him.

Pagan Prayer and Christian Prayer

*The only prayer still to be heard is not man's
prayer to God, but God's prayer to man.*

Christ showed us true power just as he showed us the true
God. He instituted a Christian prayer, as different from
pagan prayer as Jesus was from Jupiter.

After three years of living with his apostles and teaching
them, he said to them one day: "You do not know how to
pray. You have never prayed as you should. I am going to
teach you a new prayer, a prayer that will always be heard."
This gave the apostles a shock, for they had prayed much—
innumerable psalms, innumerable ceremonies.

But he taught them an inspired prayer, made in his name,
in a spirit of filial confidence, with complete assurance. Not
a prayer of whining beggars, of servants, but the prayer of
a son: "Father, I know that you always listen to what I say."
"Father, everything that is yours is mine."

Do you pray like that? Do you dare? But then how do
you dare to call him "Father"? Can you imagine a son saying to his father, "I know that you don't always listen to
me; it depends on how you're feeling. I know that some of
your things are not mine; you always keep the best things
for yourself." If you can, you do not know much about being a father!

Pagan prayer is spontaneous prayer; it is a derisory attempt to change God, to draw his attention to something to which he does not seem to be attaching quite the importance you would like him to, to move him, to warm him up like an unwilling engine, to shake him up before exploiting him.

But with God and us, there is only one party to be changed for the better, and that is us. There are a lot of Christians who would not like to be the God they imagine; they would rather be someone better. Think of all the common phrases they use about him, such as: "God gives us grace where he will, when he will," or "No one knows when God will stretch out his hand to us," or "You have to take grace when it comes or it may not come again." The *real* God suffered death to offer his grace, died from the refusal we give him—and we still think of him as someone who is capricious and indifferent.

Prayer is not talking to God, but listening to God talking to you. What do monks do for six hours a day, in the Office? They listen to the word of God, repeating it to themselves until it speaks to them and they become capable of speaking to men in words full of God.

Do our prayers "nourish" God? This is pagan—it was the idolators who fed their gods. The Christian God serves us at table and makes us eat our fill, until we become capable of feeding others in our turn.

Do you think you pray to God? No, it is God who prays to you. You can never ask God for as much as he wants to give you. You can never ask God for as much as he has already given you.

The shame of it is that nearly all of our prayers are pagan under a Christian gloss. When they were in Latin, we were sufficiently drugged by them not to notice. But today we have to wake up and think about them, and our so-called prayers, our "collects" and "post-communions," stick in our throats.

They are all in the imperative. Whether they "supplicate"

or demand, they induce in us a belief that it is God who must change, that he is the great obstacle standing in the way of the world becoming a paradise. This sort of thing: "May the innocent prayer of little children, the pure prayer of virgins, the anxious prayer of mothers, finally obtain from God the peace they all desire." But it was God who gave us peace, God is the one who desires peace! When we ask him for peace, we are merely turning back to him the request he addresses to us. Prayer is this: *our* finally opening up to what God has always been proposing to us. Men make war, and only men can make peace; you ask God for something, but he can only do it through you. Praying is letting yourselves be filled with all the longing for peace that there is in God's heart, until he can work in us. If we say: "Only a miracle can bring peace in Vietnam," it is as good as saying that the war is God's fault. Waiting for a miracle is exactly the last thing we should be doing. But we must pray in order to be filled with the desire for peace that God breathes into us.

It is a funny thing, but when one tries to tell a Christian audience that prayer changes not God, but man, they immediately conclude that they needn't pray any more. The truth is exactly the opposite: if it were God who had to be convinced by prayer, the matter would be quickly settled; but since it is us, it takes quite a bit longer. The pagan mentality is so deeply rooted in us that we find it much more stimulating (and easier) to address ourselves to God in order to make him better than to give ourselves to him so that he can change us.

Our prayers are infantile: "Lord, have mercy." Think about it: who is truly the one that lacks mercy, that should open himself to compassion, that should be implored to be merciful? When, for once, a ray of God's infinite pity, of his terrible suffering in the face of the wretchedness of the earth, reaches us and moves us, our reaction is not at all to feel responsible, to stir ourselves to go and help—no, it is to turn to God and give him the favor of our illumination, to invite him to become as good as ourselves and to beg him to take charge of just those whom he has confided to our care!

Take another example: "The Lord be with you." Think about it: do you suppose that he is not? That he is somewhere else? Who is truly the one that stays away? Do you think you can really make him come? Recall him to his duties? Rather we should say: "The Lord *is* with you. My brothers and sisters, let us, this once, be with him."

And when are we going to have a purge of the Psalms? When is a Christian poet going to discover the poetry of the New Testament? Two thousand years of sterility!

The Preface of the Apostles: "Do not abandon your Church, O Lord." Tell me who's the one truly more likely to abandon it?

"Remember, Lord, your servants . . ." Is his memory failing him perhaps, growing feeble with his great age? The truth, rather, is that only with his inspiration and in his presence that we remember those whom he has confided to us and put in our care. Should we not rather say: "Before you, because of you, Lord, we remember . . ."? And what of all those prayers asking God to "take away his wrath," to "allow us to breathe," to make us "despise the things of this world"?

I know that you are intelligent enough to grasp the meaning through the words, but the trouble is that penetrating the verbiage becomes such a demanding intellectual exercise that it takes all our attention away from praying. Why should not the prayers say what they mean directly, without cloaking it all in what they do not mean?

Christian prayer is quite different.

Prayer is offering ourselves to God so that he may have a chance of doing in us what he is always wanting to do, but is prevented from doing by our going away before he has a chance to begin. It is God who prays to men, and men who do not listen to his prayers.

Christian prayer is reminding ourselves of God's call, consenting to God's plan for us, to his proposal to us. Every Christian prayer is an act of thanking. It is never a question of counting our riches, of measuring the unbelievable extent of God's generosity—"If you but knew the gift of God . . ." Every prayer is a Eucharist, a thanksgiving, a joyful recognition (in the sense both of taking stock and of accepting) of what God is doing in us.

When we were young we learned that there were four types of prayer: adoration, thanksgiving, petition and repentance. But for me now there is only one: the Eucharist.

Adoration is recognizing that God is God—but the Christian God is the God who has given us everything. For the pagan, adoring him means saying: "I love you, I give you everything, I vow myself to your service." But for the Christian, it means recognizing his absolute generosity: "You give me everything, you are pure gift, love, self-giving. I shall never be able to know how much you love me, how much you have loved me. And when, inspired by your love, I look for something to give back to you, I find that you turn my gifts towards other men: 'Whatever you do to the least of my brethren . . .' And then you are delighted to come alive in me, to have become all in all."

Prayer of petition cannot be made without the action of grace within us; it is an acceptance of and a thanksgiving for what grace does in us. "If anyone pretend that without the inspiration of the Holy Spirit and his help, we are capable of making an act of faith, hope, charity or repentance such as is necessary for our salvation, let him be anathema," said the Council of Trent in its pre-John XXIII style. And St. Paul said: "We do not know how to pray as we ought, but the Spirit himself intercedes for us with sighs too deep for words" (Romans 8, 26). And Christ assured us that the Father knows what is good for us far better than we do.

The Collect for the Ninth Sunday after Pentecost asks: "Teach them to ask the things that please you so that you may give what they ask." Just one inspired demand, and one capable of being heard!

And prayer of repentance? Do you know that when you ask God's pardon, he is so longing to forgive you that this longing overflows from his heart into yours and in the end makes you want to be forgiven, so much does he want to forgive you? The problem is not obtaining God's pardon; the problem, for God, is making you accept his pardon. We cannot deserve it, and we cannot really even ask for it— only open ourselves to it.

But, you might say, if God always hears us, or rather anticipates us, why are so many prayers said in vain? As a child, I prayed for years to become a great saint (plain saint not being good enough . . .) and was amazed to find at the end of them that God had not made me one. Didn't he want me to be holy?

Yes, God always hears us, but in the exact measure of our sincerity. The effectiveness of our prayer is gauged by the truth of our aspiration, not by the words we pronounce. If God took us at our word when we asked for sainthood, we would be left screaming with pain, surprise and revolt; we would be yelling: "Leave me alone. You're hurting me too much. Don't touch this; that's the last thing I can give you, it's what I prize most!" And we would then understand that in asking for sanctity what we were really after was a halo, a nice coat of varnish over our faults, and the removal of a few warts from our interesting countenance. But once it becomes a question of emptying ourselves of ourselves (particularly of our ambitions to sainthood) and filling ourselves with the humility, availability and generosity of Christ, then it takes a lot of time, a lot of calls, a lot of meetings before we accept this plan of God for each of us.

Each prayer is a planing away at the thick plank of our

resistance, our mistrust, our incredulity. When will the grace that presses upon us break through?

"But Christ himself told us to pray, when he said that he who asked would receive, he who searched would find, and he who knocked would have the door opened to him. So?"

Of course, but why do we always receive? Because what we ask is already given. Why do we find? Because it is presented to us. Why can we go in? Because the door is already open. Of course we must pray, and even pray all the time, but let me ask one question: by demanding, by importuning, like the widow before the unrighteous judge in the parable (Luke 18), whose resistance do you think you are breaking down? God's resistance to giving, or your own resistance to receiving? Do we really think that God, like the judge, will be worn out by our continual importuning? If all that was needed was to persuade God to give, I assure you that it would not take long. But as it is a question of persuading us to receive, we will never see the end of it!

"But Christ himself prayed for his wants."

Yes, Christ himself began, like any one of us, by asking for things he did not need to ask for. Nearly all of his prayers are in two parts: a first in which he simply expresses his fear, his wants, his spontaneous reaction, but then a second which follows with reflection, consultation in depth, total consent, gratitude that God is God and that nothing can be better than what he gives us. At the beginning of his prayer he asks: "If it is possible, let this chalice pass from me . . ." but then he goes on: "Not my will, but thine . . ."[1] Another time he begins by saying: "Now is my soul troubled. And what shall I say? 'Father, save me from this hour?'" Then he collects himself, consults himself: "No, for this purpose I have come to this hour. Father,

[1] Let us not interpret this as the Father's will that his son should die, but the Father's proposal to remain faithful to love even on the Cross.

glorify thy name" (John 12, 27). In the same way: "In the days of his flesh, Jesus offered up prayers and supplications [that is, prayers of petition], with loud cries and tears, to him who was able to save him from death, and he was heard for his godly fear. Although he was a son, he learned obedience through what he suffered" (Hebrews 5, 7). He received so much more than he asked for: he asked to escape and received the burden to bear. But he opened himself to God's gift.

Let us pray like that—not to persuade God to do our will, but to persuade ourselves that he knows, better than we do, what is good for us, and that he is so much more anxious to give it to us than we are to accept it. Tell God what is in your mind: that is fine, a relief, but as soon as you start to reflect, as soon as you stop listening to yourself and listen to him, your prayer will change its tone and you will no longer be asking for anything except what he wants to give you.

Now liturgical prayers should be reflective prayers, instead of confirming the faithful in their pagan ways. This is why the great Christian prayers are prayers of thanksgiving (and since the Preface tells us to give thanks always and everywhere, one wonders how any other sort is ever contemplated!).

The Gloria: "We give you thanks for your great glory" —we need not invent anything greater to praise you than the memory of what you have done for us, of how much you have loved us.

The Credo: a joyous, wondering enumeration of all that God has done for us. After such a recalling of his favors (Christian prayer is a "Memorial"), we are sure that he will never lose heart, that he will never leave us, and that all we have to do is imitate him—because when we remind ourselves of his mission, we begin to realize our own.

The Benedictus and Magnificat: not a single petition in these hymns, but only an unfolding to the full realization of God's gift. The religion of what one does for God—those poor, hard, sad things one does for God: mortifications, sacrifices, privations—is pagan religion. The Greeks thought that God did not love men, that it was men who loved God. So they crawled to him to steal a little of his warmth and light (which is what we do all too often when we pray: crawl to God to wheedle something out of him). But Christianity is the religion of what God does for us, the great things, the *"mirabilia Dei,"* the marvels he does in the poverty of his servants.

Te Deum, Gloria Patri, Sanctus, Eucharistic Prayer: "It is truly right and fitting to give you thanks always and everywhere." And, in the middle of the Consecration: "He gave you thanks." All the letters of St. Paul begin with an act of thanksgiving.

Alas, Christians have lost the feeling of thanksgiving! When all our "intentions" are collected together, what do they turn out to be but a series of catastrophes: "For so-and-so who is losing his faith; for someone else whose marriage is breaking up; for three hundred children drowned; for the victims of a railway accident; for someone about to have an operation . . ." What a splendid set of things to give thanks for!

Worse still, even the Church has disfigured its Eucharist; it has tried to force the revelation of Christ into the framework of a pagan sacrifice. The prayers of the Roman Canon (of which those of the Offertory—at least before the *Missa normative*—were but an unhappy paraphrase) are essentially pagan prayers. Is the Mass above all the sacrifice of man to God, or of God to man? From the texts one would think it was we who were sacrificing ourselves to God. Who offers himself to the other: man to God or God to man? Who takes the initiative? Who *feeds* the other? Who serves the other? We have changed the gift that God makes of himself into a gift that we make to him.

God gives us his son to live in each of us and go on lov-

ing and saving men: we solemnly send him back! Return
to sender! How pleased he must be! We put ourselves in the
ridiculous position of intervening between two persons of
the Blessed Trinity in order to persuade the first to "deign"
to accept the sacrifice of the second.

All this is a revival of the pagan rituals, which center
everything on the worship of God, on man's efforts towards
him, the gifts we offer him to "appease" him. But Christianity is centered on the actions of God towards us, on the
revelation of his "*agapē*." And clearly, by opening ourselves
to God, we give ourselves to him, and by letting him serve
us we give him the sort of service he wants—which is not
that we should turn back to him and give back what he
has given to us, but that we should turn towards our
brothers.

Many people think that we should take time off from
serving men occasionally in order to devote ourselves to
God. But the whole question is surely to know whether we
are closer to him when we are following his example of
looking after our neighbor, or when we are devoting ourselves directly to God. The two commandments are in-
divisible, in the sense that when we do something for our
neighbor, we are doing it for God; but what we do for God
"alone" is not done for our neighbor.

It is pretty shattering to discover, after years of "Christian
education," that there is no such thing as "the worship of
God" in Christianity. God did not come to be served; he
came to serve. The whole novelty of Revelation is that God
"does not live in shrines made by man, nor is he served by
human hands, as though he needed anything, since he himself gives to all men life and breath and everything," as St.
Paul told the Athenians (Acts 17, 24-5).

The true worship to offer to God is to practice the service
that he gives to man, to remind ourselves, to make a
memorial of the gift he has given us. The true service of
God is letting him, once more, serve us. Could one ever in-

vent a finer form of homage to God than the constant recalling of what he has done for us? God's true "glory" does
not consist in receiving our homage, but in re-presenting,
making present among us again his gift of love and humility: "Behold, I am in your midst as a servant."

The essential message of Christianity is the revelation
that "it is not we who have loved God, but God who has
loved us," that the First has made himself the last, the Master has made himself a servant. Our "worship" should consist in realizing, remembering, giving thanks for, steeping
ourselves in this ever-new "good news." But we are so pagan
that we know better than God what is good for us; we know
the true values and impose them on him.

When the Word became flesh, he had to choose which of
all human values would be the most apt for showing God's
taste, for revealing the divine way of life. And he completely
discounted riches, honors, force, authority, glory, violence.
He chose poverty, humility, gentleness, service, suffering,
passion for justice and mercy. And we tell him: "Thanks
for the show. For thirty-three years you pretended to be
feeble, poor, humble and a servant. What an effort that must
have been, what a terrible constraint. Luckily, that's over
first; we are going to put things back in their proper pro-
portions, do things as they should be done, restore your dignity to you. Now we are going to serve you, and you are
going to be served; you are going to sit on that throne, and
we are going to humble ourselves before you; we are going
to strip ourselves for you, and you are going to sparkle with
gold and precious stones. Obviously this is the sort of glory
you want, because it's what we all want for ourselves."

This is how we have put human values in the place of
revealed divine values, and completely buffered the shock
of Revelation. Which is greater for God, to be first served
or first servant? All during my youth, I was taught to take
"God, first served" as my motto (it is Joan of Arc's); it took
me many years to understand that it is much better to say to

God: "God, first servant." God is so much more lover than beloved, so much more servant than served, so much more praying than prayed to!

The essence of the Mass is Christ putting on an apron, sitting us at his table, preparing our meal, serving the bread, giving his bread, his love, our life. And we picture him as a Master and a Lord, seated on a throne, receiving our homages, loaded with our offerings—provided we insist enough that he "deign" to accept them. Before celebrating the Eucharist, Christ took off his clothes and girded himself with a towel. And his representatives cover themselves in "ornaments."

The essence of Penance: Christ, still in his apron, kneels down to wash our feet. In this Christian liturgy, the penitent is seated and the confessor on his knees. Peter finds this intolerable: "You will never wash my feet!" The Church finds it intolerable too. So we have the priest sitting in the confessional like a judge on his bench, and instead of humbly washing the penitent's feet, interrogating him (how many times? Who with? Where? How?) and then gesturing imperiously over his head.

So God is travestied. Herod had already dressed him in purple but that was to mock him. We do it to honor him. Christ must be suffocating in our golden monstrances, our "incomparable" chalices, our jewel-encrusted ciboria—he, after all, loved the straw of the manger and the wood of the cross.

Am I trying to change everything, you might say; am I calling for a revolution? No, I just want Christ's revelation to stay a living thing, a shock of surprise, news, good news . . .

The "worshipful," pagan, Constantinian orientation of our Mass is just what prevents the faithful from feeling the impact of Christ's revelation, of his invection. If the Mass is doing things for God, then we are finished with him once it is finished. If God is a being who loves to be served, incensed, praised, nourished, fêted, then it is natural that we should aspire to become like him, and that we should find it compatible with the Gospel to be majestic, pompous, authoritarian, full of our own importance, admired and served. But if celebrating Mass is wondering at the way God loves us and serves us, then we shall become imbued with sensitivity to these values of life, love and service.

By developing a "cult" of God, which is turning back to God what he has done for us, we fall into a vicious circle which Christ did everything to break out of: he tried to teach us to love one another as he loved us. And we tell him, as a reward, that we have come to love him!

But is it not natural that after receiving so many gifts from God, we should want to do something for him in our turn? "Nothing is too much for God," declared the good Curé of Ars. Yes, but when you want to do someone a favor, whose tastes do you take into account? The sender's or the receiver's? Don't be like those husbands who give their wives birthday presents of the wonderful TV sets they have always wanted themselves. This is what we are doing to God when we offer him gold and silver, precious stones, incense and a throne. But Christ's tastes are quite plain to see. He does not ask us to love him and offer him gifts. He wants us to love each other, to show our love for him in our love for our brother. He tells us that what we do to the least of our brethren, we do to him. We can never be closer to God, more pleasing to him, more alive with him, than when we let him do in us what he likes doing: not being loved, but loving; not being served, but serving; not being honored as Master, but making himself the last of all and the servant of all.

Be careful: you will become the God you imagine. If you think that being God is being served, honored, incensed, feared, then I can see the sort of person you are at home, in your family and your community—and certain overbearing fathers and ecclesiastical dignitaries are striking images of

the God they were taught to have. But if you know that
being God is being loving, serving, kind, simple and brotherly, then you will renew the revelation of Jesus Christ.

Jesus knew who God was: "Knowing that the Father had
given all things into his hands, and that he had come from
God and was going to God," he did . . . what? What does
one do when one knows one has come from God and is
going to God? He "rose from supper, laid aside his garments
and girded himself with a towel. Then he poured water
into a basin and began to wash the disciples' feet . . ." But
Peter thought he knew it all; he knew the etiquette, the
rubrics, the "Pontifical." So he rebuked him: "Lord, do you
wash my feet?" Let us know our place! Let us keep our dignity! An old parish priest once restrained his curate who
had darted forward to pick up a parishioner's hat, with the
words, "Let's behave like priests!" What's more, Peter has
ecclesiastical ambitions; he sees a brilliant career ahead of
him: he wants to be head of the Church. So when he sees
the Lord get up, wind a towel round himself, kneel down
in front of the others, he sees his career in danger and his
job threatened. So he protests, as any one of us would, at
this reversal of values: "You shall never wash my feet!"

And then the Lord speaks the hardest of all words to
him: "If I do not wash you, you have no part in me." That
is, you will not sympathize with my tastes, you will not have
the revelation of my beatitudes, you will have nothing in
common with my character. James and John had already
wanted to call down fire from heaven on a town in Samaria
—a typical ecclesiastical procedure. But Christ was angry
with them, and told them they didn't know their mind, that
the Son of man had come to save lives, not lose them. And
to Peter, as to any one of us, he gave the terrible warning:
if you do not let me wash your feet, if you refuse the idol-
shattering shock of seeing your God at your feet, your God
washing your feet, your God getting your meals for you,
serving you at table, washing up for you—if you haven't

accepted that, suffered that, if you haven't died to your ideas, your prejudices, your etiquette, your tastes, you will never rise again to my people.

The anxious, tormented pagan, in his attempts to reach God, strives to build a vast tower of efforts, sacrifices, offerings, asceticism, mysticism. He can never do enough to appease his angry God, to touch the heart of his indifferent God, to move his unfeeling God. And his towers always collapse in pride, discouragement, quarrels. But while he is wrapped up in his mad project, God is there—kneeling before him, stripped of his garments and washing his feet, so that man may, gropingly, blindly, touch his face, stroke his forehead, know his smile and finally discover that God is not above us, but below us, that he is not waiting for us on a pedestal, but on the level of the poorest of those whose feet we wash.

I remember a concelebrated High Mass. Solemn—bishop, thirty priests, a thousand faithful. And when it came to communion, they noticed there were not enough hosts. They broke them in two, in four, in eight, but to no avail: a hundred faithful still went without communion. Afterwards, they argued about who was responsible, blamed the sacristan. Suddenly a layman spoke up: "If, for once, you hadn't helped yourselves first, there would have been enough to go round." It fell like a bomb, a thunderbolt from the Holy Spirit. But is it not true that there is nothing evangelical about the priest helping himself first? Or about the fact that there are two "sittings"—one for *me*, first, at the altar, and then one for *you*, at the rails? Christ was a simple, brotherly being: he ate with his apostles, at the same table, and waited on them. But *I*, a priest, I am a superior being, I do not share my meal with you, I have my own table, I eat at the top altar, and keep you the other side of the rails—*communion* rails!

This liturgy is not Christian, but what is the use of changing the liturgy without changing people's minds?

When we start having "community" masses with people who feel no sense of community, we lie even more than before. If Christians were to rediscover that their God is the simplest, humblest, most pliant of beings, then perhaps the priest would stop serving himself before the others. "If, for once, you hadn't helped yourselves first, there would have been enough to go round."

Note. The Roman Canon, even in the new translation, which has been attacked as "stripping it of its mystery" and so on, still retains too many of the pompous, redundant, Constantinian, Sun-King phrases of the Latin: glory and majesty, altar in heaven, honor, look with favor . . . ; too many devalued images, endless blessings, illogicalities (asking that those now at rest may find peace), conclusions that do not conclude, puerilities (save us from final damnation), too much exclusivity—only Christians are prayed for, and its peremptory tone: accept this, remember that, do the other . . .

✧ II ✧

A God You Would Be Glad to Pray to

*Prayer is not talking to God but
listening to God talking to you.*

Prayer is not asking things of God, but receiving what he
wants to give you; it is not being heard by God, but hearing
God praying to you; it is not asking God's forgiveness, but
opening yourself to his forgiveness; it is not offering yourself to God, but welcoming God offering himself to you.

So what does prayer really amount to? It amounts to paying attention to God praying in us, forgetting our needs,
our rebellions, our hopes, consenting to God's unfolding of
his plans for us.

"Everything that you ask in my name will be granted to
you." If you have not received, it is because you have not
prayed in the right way.

But isn't it just mystification to pretend that God hears
us when we ask him for what he wants to give us?

Do you really want anything else? Wouldn't that be
claiming to know better than he what is good for you? All
prayer is a response: you cannot talk to God unless he has
already addressed his Word to you; if he has not spoken to
you, you have nothing to say to him. You cannot get in
touch with him unless he has already got in touch with
you. You cannot invoke God unless he has already con-

voked you. You cannot give him thanks unless he has already given you something to thank him for.

Do you want to do something for God that he has not already done for you? This would be trying to be better than God. *You would then be denying him in the act you thought was recognizing him.*

But have you anything to thank him for? Do you know a God you would like to talk to, imitate, live in? You will never pray unless you are glad to do so, which means that the only God you can pray to is one who has revealed himself to be so much better than you ever imagined, a God who makes you give thanks for his very existence. This is how prayer sprang from Christ's heart: "Father, I bless you . . . Father, I give you thanks . . . Father of justice, the world has not known you, but I have known you!" We have nothing to ask of a God like this; we just have to stay in his presence long enough to let ourselves be filled with him.

Have you had such a revelation from God?

Unfortunately, our idea of God tends to be constantly downgraded. As soon as one tries to hang on to it, as soon as one fails to renew it, to refresh it at its source in Revelation, it congeals, dries up, shrinks, becomes a caricature, a scarecrow, an idol. All our natural ideas of God are idols. Men have been so wrong about God that he had to come and tell them who he was: "No one has ever known God . . . It is the Son who has revealed him."

Idolatry is not a specialty of primitive civilizations—it is a modern industry: we are idol factories. If one could extract all our false ideas about God from our brains and collect them together, one would have the finest ethnographic museum in the world, a fantastic collection of totems, taboos and demons.

Most men feel guilty before God; they are frightened of him because they think of him as cross, grumbling and supercilious. This does not stem from individual peculiarities, but has a universal explanation: God made man in his image and likeness and now we have gone and done the same to him! There is no stopping us from imagining God as what we would like to be—majestic, lordly, fearsome . . . And then, since we are not very happy with him like this, we think he cannot be very happy with us! As we then don't like to think about him too much, we assume that he doesn't want to bother too much about us. And as we cannot love him very much, we tend to think that he cannot love us very much either!

But the whole of Revelation teaches us that God is not like us at all, that if we want to know how he feels about us, the last thing to do is think how we feel about him. God loves us when we do not love him; he doesn't need us to love him to make him love us. God doesn't love us because we are worthy of his love, but he goes on loving us so tenderly and patiently that in the end we shall become worthy of it.

There is nothing more pharisaical than wanting to be worthy of God's love before understanding that he loves us unworthy, than trying to compete with God in loving before experiencing his love. And there are two sorts of pharisees: the pharisee who thinks it is his right to be loved because he deserves it—he prays, he makes offerings, he makes sacrifices, he goes to church . . . ; and the pharisee in reverse who thinks he cannot be loved because he doesn't deserve it. Both live by the pharisaical principle that one is loved if one deserves to be; it is only their application of the principle that differs.

But Christianity is the good news that God loves the unworthy, that he does not need us to be worthy in order to love us. And the consequence is vital: you will behave like your God. If you wait for your brothers to become worthy of being loved, you will wait for the rest of your life. Because they are waiting for you to love them so that they can be worthy of your love. They need to be loved if they are to become better. What we have to do is love our brothers so much that they become lovable.

"No one has ever known God." One only knows God by chance, by grace, by surprise, by revelation—and not a revelation put in cold storage for two thousand years, but a continuing, immediate, personal revelation, a present-day Pentecost. "Without vision the people shall perish" is as true today as it was at the time of the prophets of Israel.

There is a sign that you know God: you suddenly realize you have never known him—this is seeing the truth. There is a sign that you are beginning to know what faith is: you are frightened how little you live it—this gives you a point of comparison with what went before. And there is a sign that you are really praying: "I have never prayed like this"— now you know what it is. And a sign that you have met someone very great: you suddenly feel very small, and happy with it—as long as you are pleased with yourself, proud of your behavior, satisfied with your religious knowledge (the pharisees had patented their knowledge of God's ways), you can be sure you have never met anyone very great.

No man can hand on revelation; no one can give you a dispensation from the Holy Spirit. The inner witness of the Spirit, now just as much as two thousand years ago, is the only way to know God. Only God knows how to talk about God. God can be more unknown in his Church than outside it ("The harlots and publicans go before you . . .") because knowing about God can easily take the place of knowledge of God. Dogmas give a dispensation from faith. Faith only serves to hold us up to God, waiting, discovering, wondering. Faith is openness to revelation.

Christianity is just as new, just as revolutionary today as when it started. It is such a shock to common sense, to spontaneous convictions, to traditional religion, that we haven't been able to stand it and have done our best to re-paganize it. Jesus did not come to start a religion, in the sense of an

organization with a number of specialized actions and
specialized persons to put us in touch with God: his greatest
liberation is to have liberated us from religion! He wanted
us all to have free, direct and joyful access to God, easy and
happy communication with him. Christianity is made for
lay people, people who belong to the world in the fullest
sense, who adore God in spirit and in fact, who give thanks
always and everywhere. It doesn't need priests to monopo-
lize the priesthood: all are priests; it doesn't need temples:
we are temples; it needs no other rites than the commonest
everyday rites: sharing food and sharing forgiveness. And
that is what we all have to do.

Christ did everything not to belong to the priestly caste
of his day, to be a layman living the life of the simple people, of fishermen and sinners, to be a man like other men,
the Son of man. And we have managed to reconstitute
a clerical set-up as exclusive, authoritarian and oppressive as
that which finally executed him!

But his greatest revolution is the revelation of God. Christ
is the Copernicus of religion: before him, everything re-
volved around the worship of God—how to appease God,
how to find favor with him, how to calm our fears by giving
him his ration of honors, gold and blood. Christ made everything revolve round the service of man. True worship of
God is respect for man. The pagan asks: "How do I find
favor with God?", and Christ replies: "Find favor with your
brother, be kind to him."

For the pagan, everything is sacred: the Temple, the altar, the vessels; there are Holy Places to go to on pilgrimage
—woods, springs, hillsides. Everything, that is, except man:
monkeys and cows are sacred, and men die of hunger beside these "temples of God." But for Christ, man alone is
sacred, and everything else is at his service—*even God!*

"These words are too hard; who can accept them?" But
if you believe that God is love, how can you not believe that
he is service? God is love, but love is dependence; God de-

pends on men far more than men on God—because he loves
them so much more than they love him. Don't dismiss this
as just paradox: it is the heart of Christianity, and he who
will not accept it is incapable of being a Christian: "The
infinitely loving is infinitely poor, infinitely humble, infinitely dependent" (Père Varillon).

Who depends more on the other: parents on their children, or children on their parents? Let mothers and fathers
reply: Of course children depend on their parents on the
level of everyday life—for authority, education, money . . .
but parents depend on their children on the level of love—
and which level is the higher? What is the children's future? To free themselves from their parents. What is the
parents' future? To remain available to their children . . .
and their grand-children.

Yes, we depend on God on the level of everyday life—for
grace, for forgiveness . . . but God depends on us on the
level of love—he loves us so much more than we love him.
Look at your crucified God—there he is: dependent, bound,
tied down, subjected. Look at yourself: free to go away, to
do what you want—the one who loves less is always stronger!

God has far more need of us than we have of him. We
are everything to God; God is nothing without us. Or you
don't know what love is.

There is nothing more pagan than the catechism answer:
"God made the world for his glory . . ." The infinite egoist
who refers everything to himself! His glory in fact consists
in loving: he made the world to show just how far he loved
us, suffered in us, hoped in us.

There is nothing more pagan than the beginning of the
Spiritual Exercises of St. Ignatius: "Man was created to
praise, love and serve God, and so [!] to save his soul." Can
you imagine a father having children to praise him and
serve him? If you think that is what yours are going to do,
you're in for a fine time with the young people of today!

Obviously, the reverse is true. You have children to love

them and serve them so well that one day they may be capable of loving and serving like you. But not loving and serving *you*—rather loving and serving others, becoming fathers and mothers in their turn. Then you will have truly carried out and handed on your parenthood. If you brought your children up for yourselves, then you would be denying your parenthood in your practice of it: your children would become your parents, your benefactors. But by bringing them up to become parents in their turn, you spread your parenthood across the world. And do you think God is less capable of doing this than we are? Why this everlasting desire to re-paganize him back into a tyrant and profiteer?

God created man to love and serve this man so well that he in his turn will become capable of loving and serving his brothers. So that man might become a father, become love, become God. God created the world to let loose a flood of love that would engulf the whole world. God shows himself through you if God in you loves your brothers much better than if God in you loves himself. The Father's joy is in being handed on to his children so well that they love each other with his love.

It is the constant temptation of the pious to believe that filial love can only be expressed and achieved in a deliberate turning back towards the Father, in calling on him and acting towards him in a way distinct from our dealings with our neighbors in ordinary brotherly love. But this is missing the unity of the two commandments. How can we think that the Father is only satisfied if, at particular moments, the love he has taught us is turned back on him alone? Are we more "of the Father" when we think explicitly of him, or when we give ourselves over entirely to the promptings of love he puts in our hearts? Isn't love of the Father totally expressed in loving our neighbor with the Father's own love? Why should we have to stop loving others for a moment in order to love him properly?

"If anyone says, 'I love God,' and hates his brother, he is

a liar; for he who does not love his brother whom he has seen, cannot love God whom he has not seen" (1 John 4, 20). But can anyone really love his brother and hate God? Love for God can be illusory, but love for one's brother is a verifiable fact. So in Christianity the show of love for one's brother takes precedence over the show of filial love: "Go first and be reconciled to your brother . . ."

You will never know any God other than the one you become. You will never know God except by becoming, literally or figuratively, a Father. You will only know love by loving. Love is not made to be loved, but to be loving: it is through being amazed at the love you can feel for another person that you first know the wonder of the love God has always felt for you. "As for me, it's when I became a father that I understood what that means: to be God" (Balzac, *Père Goriot*).

You must not love God, but live him; it's awful to love love. God is not the object of your love; he is the driving force behind it. God is not a rival suitor for man's love for his fellow men; he is the substance of it. He does not want to be one of his creatures; he wants to be all in all, a total presence, an Epiphany of love through the sacrament of humanity. You have to do far more for God than love him: you have to let him become flesh in you, let yourself be divinized by him, let him love in you. God is a life you live with, a love you love with, a current going through you, a gale blowing you towards others.

Just how Christian is that sentence of St. Augustine's that so charmed the piety of our younger days: *"Fecisti nos ad te, Domine, et irrequietus est cor nostrum donec requiescat in Te"*—"Thou hast made us for Thyself, O Lord, and our heart is restless until it rest in Thee." What father begets children for himself? What would you think of parents whose sons or daughters could say to them: "You have brought us up for your own sake; we are only happy with

you; there's no place like home." And what would their
sons-in-law and daughters-in-law think of them?

Just how Christian is the rule of St. Benedict: *"Opus Dei,
nil praeferatur"*—that is, let nothing be put before the
Sacred Office, the worship of God. This would make God a
vampire of men. There is no worship of God in Christianity; anything that has to do with the service of man should
be put before the worship of God! "Go first and be reconciled with your brother"; "Learn what this word means: I
want mercy and not burnt offerings"; "There is one sign
that we have passed from death to life: that we love the
brethren." Luckily, even in Benedictine monasteries, the
infirmarian stays with the sick, the porter welcomes trav-
ellers, and the cook stays by his oven—even during the
Office! But it seems that we have only pagan formulas in
which to express Christianity. And this new wine ferments
and makes the old bottles explode.

Christ announced that the grandiose worship in the Temple of Jerusalem was finished, that it would be replaced by
a spiritual worship (in spirit and truth), that the Temple
would be destroyed and replaced by his Body, built of living
stones. But all that has remained a dead letter; we have built
millions of temples in which to celebrate millions of "worships." Christ was killed because he said: "Destroy this
Temple and I will build it up again in three days." He was
speaking of the Temple of his Body, as the evangelist points
out. St. Paul was arrested in the Temple because he
"preached ceaselessly against the Holy Places and against
the Law" and because he proclaimed that God "does not
live in shrines made by man." And what did St. Stephen
say? That the Temple of Jerusalem and its worship were
outdated; that the commandment was not to go to church, to
frequent the Temple, but, "Love one another," "Respect
man."

To the "religious" mentality all that is sacrilegious and
blasphemous—today just as much as in those days, alas! St.

Stephen was attacking the Law and the Holy Place. But when a traditionally formed Christian confesses today, it is nearly always to offenses against the Holy Place ("I have missed Mass on Sundays") and against the Law (fasting and abstinence, holydays of obligation, regular prayers). The average Christian confesses exclusively about "worship"—paganism, that is.

Christ would still be killed today: he would only have to say in modern terms what he said to his contemporaries. His most revolutionary word was probably: "The Sabbath is made for man, not man for the Sabbath." Try going into any church today and saying:

"God is at man's service, not man at God's.

"The Mass is to serve men, not men to serve the Mass.

"Sunday is made for man, not man for Sunday.

"A church is made for men, not God. It is the house of men, not the house of God. The priest's job is not to serve God, but to serve men.

"You have no duties to God, but you have the duty to yourselves to let God serve you and feed you so well that you become capable of sharing your bread as joyfully as he has shared his with you."

They would throw you out!

And yet you cannot proclaim Revelation well unless it is a revelation, you cannot announce the Good News properly unless it is good and new—and how can you be faithful to Christ without causing the sort of scandal he did?

Let us sum up:

The Mass is not "obligatory." Who can have made the Church out to be a wicked stepmother telling her children: "You will come and visit me for one hour each week. It doesn't much matter whether you speak or keep quiet, or whether you eat or just sit still in front of your plate—I don't care about that, but if you don't come and see me, I shall kill you!" A fine image of a Church that has grown to resemble the God it preaches!

No, you are not obliged to go to Mass on Sundays: you *are* obliged to feed yourself, and so to find a Mass that serves you, a nourishing Mass!

"I will never miss Sunday Mass!" Unfortunately, then, you will have every chance of never learning to love, because love only grows in freedom and wonderment. Understand this: if you "fulfill your duties towards God," you will never have the joyous revelation that it is God who fulfills his service towards you, who will never be filled with emotion at the servanthood, the humility, of God, who, as at the Last Supper, makes you become his *friends,* because he has taught you all that he has learnt from his Father—to love and to serve. Have you become God's friend at Sunday Mass —or just "presented your compliments" to him?

You do not go to the Eucharist to serve God; you go to learn how God breaks bread, so that you can go and do it in the same way, because God is known in the breaking of bread.

You go to the sacrament of Penance to learn the way God forgives sins, the way only God can forgive sins, in you and through you.

And in prayer, you let all the love, pity, compassion, solidarity with the sufferings of others that God inspires in you well up inside you—and only God can love the world so much as to send his son (that's you) into the world to save it. Prayer is learning God's love for man from God himself.

Church: The pagans called their temples "the house of God." I don't know if you have ever been to a pagan temple. The sanctuary is very small, because only God lives there—the unworthy public being kept at a distance. It is also very rich to honor the godhead in a manner befitting his station. The temple is built in the middle of the city, so that the god will bestow his favors and protection on it.

But a Christian church is far from being the "house of God"; it is the house of the people, a house of prayer, an assembly of the faithful. God has only one dwelling place:

you. The only holy place is man. "He has gone to stay with a sinner!" By calling the church the house of God, you profane man. By clericalizing—concentrating the sacred in particular places or people—you de-Christianize. If God really lives in a pile of bricks, then man becomes a deserted temple. But Christ died, St. Stephen was stoned, the Apostles were persecuted, because they declared that "God does not live in shrines made by man" (Acts 7, 48; 17, 24).

One only has to listen to the vehemence with which the first Christians, freed from the Temple and idols, defended the sacredness of man: "Do you not know that you are God's temple, and that God's spirit dwells in you? If anyone destroys God's temple, God will destroy him. For God's temple is holy, and that temple you are" (1 Corinthians 3, 16–17).

The exaggerated cult of the Blessed Sacrament tends to turn our churches into pagan temples. If Christ's preferred place of residence is the Blessed Sacrament, this disqualifies man. But the sacrament is at the service of man, not man at the service of the sacrament. The Eucharist means that God's only wish is to live in man: it should be used to consecrate man, and we have used it to humiliate him.

Bishops spend whole days consecrating bricks and mortar —consecrating churches *and* altars, not to mention reconsecrating them once they have been profaned!—whereas the only holy place is man and it is only the presence of the faithful that makes God present in our churches. Our concept of a church has become completely re-paganized, like so many other things. We have remade Christ's revolution— backwards. We build churches in the same spirit as the pagans built temples. They are monuments to pride, riches and waste: who else would think of putting up buildings costing hundreds of thousands that are used for less than half a day per week?

The Church should be serving and poor. The chief characteristic of a servant, as Robinson has pointed out, is that he does not live in his own house. Christ was poor, and when he wanted a room to celebrate the Last Supper, he borrowed it. But we build as though these were still the Middle Ages. Then, the church really was the people's house: it was assembly hall, fairground, museum, theatre, concert hall, even hospital for the poor. Even at the beginning of this century, the poor in some countries regarded vespers as a popular entertainment, like the cinema. That's all changed now. Now, most people don't feel at home in church. Only a tiny fraction of the population goes into one. Putting one up in the center of a town or district now is just presumption because the church is no longer the center of people's interests, and our imperialism merely offends them.

Before building a church, we should sound out opinion in the area, find out what its real requirements are, what people really need, how we can really provide a "house for the people." Do you need a swimming pool, a basketball pitch, a youth club, a cinema, a meeting hall? All right: we Christians need a room where we can meet for a few hours each week. So why don't we share?

Churches would then once again be at the service of the people, a visible sign of the sacrament of the love and goodness of Christ, who let sinners and little children come to him. They would stop being an insult to the poverty of the world, and become Christian once more. There would then be a chance that men might become Christians too.

At present, the Church is an organization avowedly at the service of the people, but which in fact devotes 90 per cent of its budget to its internal administration! What would people say if the office of Social Security were run on the same lines, with all its funds going to pay its employees and build palaces for them to work in for a few hours each week?

When the Church is rich and powerful, it disfigures Jesus Christ. He came as a poor man, and the Church is ashamed of this fact and covers him up under the attributes of Jupiter and the imperial purple of Constantine. Jesus Christ made himself poor to teach us to love and help the poor, and we rob the poor to enrich Jesus Christ!

Priests: The pagan priest was vowed to the service of his god. Jesus Christ vowed us to the service of men. God keeps nothing for himself and sends those who give themselves to him to others, to bring them the good news of man's freedom and dignity. The pagan priest was a mediator and busied himself with putting man in contact with God and God in contact with man through a series of complicated negotiations. But the first concern of the priest of Christ is revelation of the fact that God already loves us, was made flesh for us and is living amongst us, in us.

We honor our priests by incensing them, placing them on presidential chairs, serving them first . . . But the only honor a priest needs is being allowed to do his job: to be last of all and the servant of all. He is supposed to be a "representative" of Jesus Christ! But a representative would have to be someone who makes the Lord present in our midst once more, and this presence cannot be authentic unless it is humble, poor, serving, brotherly.

How can we make Christ present in our midst? We inexorably bring out the purple, the throne, the incense, the decorations, the candles—and all we make present is an idol. But the astounding presence of Christ at Mass is in the fact that he puts on an apron, washes our feet, seats us at the table and serves us while he stands! Are we astounding the world with this presence?

"Only a serving God, only a suffering God, can save" (Bonhoeffer). Man, in his misery, is always tempted to invent a God who will be compensation for his insufficiencies and fulfillment of his desires. Because man is poor, he imagines a rich God, he wants a rich God. Because man suffers, God can only be invulnerable, impassive, unfeeling and unalterable. And because man is dependent and solitary, he likes to imagine God as solitary and independent.

But this leaves man a permanent prey to his own worst ambitions and basest desires: if he is to become God, he has to become rich, strong, powerful, feared, served, self-sufficient, invulnerable—demonical!

And the Christian revelation frees and saves man through the revelation of a God who is humble, gentle, poor and merciful. It says: I have good news for you, I have a Gospel to proclaim to the world: if you are to become like God, to become God, you don't have to become rich, powerful, clever, well mannered, majestic; all you have to do is love a little more, serve a little more. You can become God all at once, in your class, at your level, just by making yourself the last of all and the servant of all.

Your most ordinary actions are the most sacred ones you perform, because the sacred is to be found far more in your life than in churches. When you come out of church you go into the Church where you give thanks always and everywhere. The true Eucharist is celebrated in your house. Every time you share food or forgiveness, this is a sacrament, an outward sign of God. Don't think your service of God is finished with a few occasional ceremonies, but learn that you are summoned to perpetuate God's revelation by repeating his gestures of love, sharing and forgiving throughout the whole world. Then we shall see his "glory"—not the glory we have foolishly forced on him in accordance with our own tastes, but the glory he chose to love "even to the death of the cross."

✧ III ✧

Praying by Listening
to the Word of God

*Praying is allowing God
to become God in us.*

Prayer is the time of God's Incarnation in you, the time
when you let yourself be inspired, when you let yourself be
transformed in his image, the time for you to learn what he
is like through seeing what you become. The instrument
with which God sculpts you into his shape in his Word.
Praying, once again, is not talking to God, but listening to
him talking to us. So learning to pray is learning to listen.

So few people know how to listen: most conversations are
criss-crossing monologues. When Solomon asked for wisdom, God gave him "a listening heart." Are you more listening heart or chattering mouth? How many husbands
listen to their wives, wives to their husbands, parents to
their children, children to their parents? And who listens
to God?

I have heard so many discouraged Christians say: "The
trouble is, when I pray, it's always just me talking. God
doesn't answer." And yet Christ said it was the pagans who
thought they could make themselves heard by sheer weight
of words . . . One never prays without a Word of God:
prayers like the "Our Father" are words of God which we repeat often enough, and I hope calmly enough, to listen to

God talking to us through them. Obviously, when we pray spontaneously, we start by saying something, anything; but if we are really listening to God, we end up being led "where we had no wish to go." We only put the words of our prayer forward, and we need supernatural tact to listen for what we should say and how to say it.

"Likewise the Spirit helps us in our weakness, for we do not know how to pray as we ought" (remember Christ's warning: "The Father knows better than you what is good for you") "but the Spirit himself intercedes for us with sighs too deep for words. And he who searches the hearts of men . . ." (He searches hearts in the sense that he sees them and digs into them. He cultivates us so that we may come to know what we really want. It is not easy to know what one really wants, and it usually is not what one says first. One has to dig down to discover that what one really wants is not what one wanted, but what one did not want!) To take up St. Paul again: "And he who searches the hearts of men knows what is the mind of the Spirit, because the Spirit intercedes for the saints according to the will of God" (what the Spirit asks, and brings us to ask, is what God wanted to give) (Romans 8, 26–7).

"They are sons of God who are led by the Spirit of God" —we do not pray unless we are inspired; we are not sons, heirs, heard, unless we pray under the guidance of the Spirit. "You have received the spirit of adoptive sons of God which makes us cry out: Abba, Father!"—if we are to say "Father" with justification, if we are to "dare" to say the first phrase of the "Our Father," we have to be inspired, indwelt by the spirit of sonship. Those who listen to the Word, or repeat it, need the same grace as those who first spoke it. Holy Scripture, the inspired book, can only be understood under the guidance of the very Spirit who inspired it. If it were not so, it would be a dead letter—the letter that kills. The same Spirit who created the word has constantly to breathe new life and meaning into it for it to talk to us.

So there are two ways of listening to or saying the same word: it can be said like a human word, like our words—and I can assure you that it is quite possible to say: "Thy will be done" while thinking only of ours!—or we can let ourselves learn how to say it. "The Spirit witnesses to our spirit that we are children of God"—there is a witness of the Spirit to tell you that you have taken up the stance of a son, that you are no longer either rebels or orphans, emancipated or wild, but that a cry that shakes you wells up from your heart—"Father!"

Learning to pray under the guidance of the Holy Spirit is an art that requires a whole course of study.

Our greatest sin is thoughtlessness: we do not know or think about the meaning or the greatness of what we are doing. "Father, forgive them, for they know not what they do" is an excuse, but also an accusation, particularly against those who claim the benefits of a Revelation, an illumination from the Holy Spirit. A poet has said: "Life must be sung." Man's greatest need is indeed to be shown the meaning of his life, the beauty of things, the presence of other beings, the infinite richness of life desired by even the dullest of men—and of which he is capable when treated with enough love and respect. Without poetry, music, and art, life would be purely utilitarian and intolerable. Today, song writers do what they can to fill the need; their songs sing of the true life for which we are made as best they can, but their longing is mixed with despair.

It would, however, be even truer to say: "Life must be prayed." Without praying, we shall never find Revelation, wonderment, thanksgiving; we shall never learn how great God is, even in our littleness.

God is in you, as he is in every creature; waiting to be guessed at, prayed to, listened to, so that he can grow in you. God is in you, and your life should be sung, should be prayed, for you to realize its dimension of eternity—all the love you can put into your most ordinary everyday actions. In olden times, armies took poets, bards, priests, troubadours, druids, chroniclers with them: all apparently useless hangers-on who in fact performed an essential task—to remind the soldiers regularly of the greatness of their exploits. Without hearing their deeds sung, the poor men-at-arms would soon have been incapable of fighting well; they would lose their pride, their *élan*, their courage, their sense of the meaning of what they were doing.

Prayer relates our doings to God himself; it links them with Jesus Christ; it ties them to the great current of love, freedom, and hope which is to change the world.

"But what do we have to do to hear God? You say that God talks to us, that his joy is making himself known in us. But we can't hear him; we can't pray; all we can do when we pause for a moment is think how tired we are. All we hear are the sounds of silence; the only thing we feel is our loneliness."

How can you believe that God loves you and yet think he does not talk to you? Loving is communicating: if God loves you, he talks to you. The very fact of revelation is an indication of his purpose. If revelation tells me that God talks to me, I already know what he is saying to me. What? That he loves me. If it tells me that God loves me, then I also know that he is going to talk to me.

It is of course not enough to believe that God once talked to us, two thousand years ago, and that he has been silent ever since because the "deposit" of Revelation was complete with the death of the last apostle! If God is not talking to us now, he never did. Because if he does not love us now, he never loved anyone.

Why do you believe that he talks to you and loves you today—because others have told you, and others told them, and so on back? But what if someone along the line made it up, told a lie, or just was too silly to understand the truth?

It's quite possible. So whom do you believe; how do you reach God?

Surely you believe because you know that the Holy Spirit is constantly repeating what Christ said to us, and constantly giving us a deeper understanding of it?

Nor is it enough to believe that he talks to a few chosen spirits, a few specialists in monasteries or the mass media. No, if he doesn't talk to everyone, including you, he doesn't talk to anyone. If he doesn't love you, he doesn't love anyone. More: you must not just "believe" that he talks to you; you must have experienced it. Faith rests on experience: without experience of God, how can you believe in him?

Too many Christians have been led astray by a false interpretation of Christ's rebuke to St. Thomas: "Blessed are those who have not seen, and yet have believed." They take it as a recommendation to try not to see, as if the less one saw, the more meritorious it was to believe—a nonsense that opens the way to every sort of credulity.

It is dishonest to believe without having seen. A little girl of seven—at that splendid age when one is still capable of thought, before the vice of religious education has squeezed out all spontaneity and curiosity—asked her pious parents: "How do you expect me to believe in Jesus? I don't know him." How sensible! Would you expect me to come and talk about someone you don't know, praise him to the skies, and then say: "Now believe in him"? Unless you were a fideist of the most extreme sort, you would reply: "I'll believe in him when I know him." And after some months of inquiry, work, and observation, you might come back to me and say: "Now I believe in him, because I know him." Which amounts to saying: "Because of what I know about him, I'm prepared to take his word for what I don't know."

And this is obviously what Thomas should have done: he knew Christ well enough, he had lived close to him for long enough, to know that this was just the sort of thing he would do—something so good, so happy, so amazing! He had already seen enough to be able to believe. Faith rests on experience, and the trouble with Christians is that most of the time their faith gets in the way of their experiencing things for themselves. They believe . . . in the faith of others. But this is believing in men, not in God; they believe in what they have been told about God, not in God himself. So many Christians believe in their parents, their pastors, their religion . . . Which dispenses them from knowing God well enough to believe in him.

"But surely we can only know God through others?"

Fine, but only you can tell if it really is God you are getting to know through others! Can we, can you, say that you know God, that he has talked to you, that you know he has talked to you? Unless you know that he has, you have no right to believe that he will again. Because once you have heard him, you know that he has always been talking to you, and that if you couldn't hear him, it was because you were not listening.

And once you have heard him, you can go and tell everyone the good news that if you can hear him, everyone can.

A Christian is someone who witnesses to the fact that God has spoken to him. This is the very definition of the Christian: he is someone whom God has called, someone whom God has spoken to, someone who is called to be a Christian, militant and prophetic, someone whom God has made me want to act like him, someone whom God has shown his preferences to—his preferences for the poor and the humble, the weak and the oppressed, for justice and mercy, for man. When you know God's tastes, they mean so much to you that you no longer want to have any others. And that's an experience, isn't it?

If you look at your life—the fact that you are reading this book, for a start, the fact that you are still a Christian, though perhaps you have moved away from Christianity at some stage and then back to it—and all the varied circumstances and sequences of events that go to make it up, can't you see the pattern of a calling, a faithfulness, a plan in it? This is God talking, and he talks to us all the time, though it is difficult to make Christians understand this. And yet they are sent into the world only to say: "I have not come of myself; it is the Father who sent me. I can do nothing by myself; it is the Father in me who works in me. It is not I who live, but Christ lives in me. His strength shows itself in my weakness."

When God speaks, men know his voice: "No one has ever spoken like this man." Then they feel at peace, strengthened and purified; they see themselves as they never have before—not very pretty, but they can now accept that fact and be glad of it, because he who makes them see themselves also makes them able to accept themselves. This sudden lucidity is not discouraging because it shows more than our faults: it also enables us to see the glow of love, the merciful radiance in which we are all bathed.

Even those who do not know God sometimes recognize him suddenly in the presence of a truly religious person, happening, or event. They are suddenly forced to say: "There is God." Why? Because God is not a philosophical concept, but someone who talks to us as no one has ever talked to us before. Then we know our inner geography; we know where things hit us. God talks to us at a level in ourselves that we ourselves cannot reach, so deep down that he himself has to make the place where he shows himself, in an inner dimension that we did not know we possessed until he declared himself in it. "The man who is of God hears the Word of God. It is because you are not of God that you do not hear his words." "My sheep know my voice and follow me."

God speaks to everyone, all the time, and no one is beyond the reach of his voice. If I have been able to give you some idea of how he talks and how to listen to him, you will know that he has already spoken a great deal to you. To be a saint, all you have to do is welcome and remind yourself of the signs you receive from God. But we hardly take any notice of them at the time, and forget them straightaway. No other person can put you in contact with God; another person can only remind you of all the times God has spoken to you. The rest is up to you, up to each one of us on his own.

✦ IV ✦

Seeing Our Lives in
the Light of the Gospel

God speaks in his Word, but also in our life.

God speaks to us through his Word, but he also speaks to us through the events of our life. Not that he "sends" us events in our lives, as the providentialists think (more about them in the next chapter): God is neither a space technician nor a sort of universal schoolmaster: we are free. But whatever we do, even sin, is an occasion for a grace, a proposal, a call from God, a call to believe and love whatever happens.

Praying is taking stock of the words which God addresses us in his Book, but it is also listening to what he has to say to us about the facts of our existence.

Being Christian is believing that life has a meaning, that everything, even sin, can turn to our benefit if we are not discouraged from loving. Not that we necessarily know the meaning—God's message is difficult to decipher, and our decoding techniques have to be constantly brought up to date. One has to pay attention to the message, scrutinize it carefully, verify it constantly. One has to be as prudent in interpreting the meaning as one is sure that there is one. And prayer is the moment when one lives one's faith in this sense, when one tries to make out the message. It is the place for the discernment of spirits, for sorting what is from God out from what is not from him.

There are two stupid attitudes that one can take to any word from God, whether it be in text or happening. The first is: "I know it all; it's crystal-clear; I've been called; God has spoken to me." As soon as you feel like that, be careful. It is the sign of a credulous and superficial nature, at once changeable and obstinate. The enthusiastic crowds on Palm Sunday were certainly made up of the same people as the bloodthirsty mob on Good Friday. Because if you have the evidence, immediately, that this thing comes from God, there is a risk of having the evidence, a moment later, that it didn't after all. The second attitude is: "I don't understand a word of it. It's all meaningless. Everything's against me. My life is a mess. What have I done to deserve this?" And there is a deep connection between the two: there is no worse sceptic than the disillusioned believer, no worse pessimist than the disillusioned optimist.

There is only one sensible course to take between the two, and that is the one Mary took, after Jesus had been missing for three days in the Temple: though she did not understand his reasons, she "kept all these things in her heart." An infinitely refreshing comment that should be applicable to all of us. After three days of wondering why her son "treated her so" came the fourth when they found him and she understood even less. For us, it might be three days or three years. Do not worry. The life of faith is like that.

Faith is saying, not "I understand," but "I will understand"; faith is not declaring: "I've got it; I see what it means," but telling oneself: "I believe there is a meaning." What the meaning is, I do not rush to define, because experience has taught me that I can never see it till later—Jesus told Peter: "What I am doing you do not know now, but afterward you will understand" (John 13, 7). This is what I like most about Mary's reaction. She and Joseph had been "astonished." She, like us, had been astonished, stupefied, totally thrown by this Word of God in her life, but she "kept all these things in her heart." If only we could keep them in the same way. Not say either "How frightful" or "How marvellous," but simply suspend judgment, wait patiently, test it, say: "This thing has a meaning, even if I can't see what it is, I've often found that things clear themselves up for me in time, so I've every reason to think that time will throw light on this. Since I usually end up understanding and appreciating what initially put me out, I'm right in thinking that what is obscure now will one day become clear."

Faith has enough light to accept its darknesses, enough certainties to bear its questions. It knows the person it believes in well enough to know that its patience is justified. But it never resigns itself to not understanding: mystery is not a wall to bang one's head against but a sea into which one plunges deeper and deeper. God has not revealed "mysteries" as a test of our faith; he has revealed truths as food we can never exhaust. And it is precisely here that the Gospel can help us to decipher our lives.

What is the Gospel? It is the story of the experience, reflected on later, of a group of men who lived our life, the same life as we live, as joyful and as gloomy: they lived with God, ate and drank with him, saw him and heard him, conversed with him and worked with him, and something in them prevented them from recognizing him, from really knowing who he was, really rejoicing at the fact. It was only later, thinking it over, letting his words ring in their ears, re-enacting his actions, putting themselves back in his presence, that they came gradually to realize, more and more fully, what had happened to them. Then they never tired of remembering, re-living, interpreting. They had made a religious reading of their lives and understood in wonder what they had lived in darkness.

We too eat, drink, move, and work with our God. We live the same adventure as the apostles, in the same ignorance. But the light of their experience can illuminate our own.

The learned works of exegetes leave us more and more

perplexed about the historical character of the sacred writings. Even while they claim to preserve the substance intact, they make us aware of so many accretions that we despair of really reaching Christ through the intermediaries who have handed him down to us. But this, which seems to separate him from us, is for me precisely what binds us more closely to him: I feel in closer communion with the facts as lived by the evangelists in their inspired meditation than with a mere historical record of events. Because I know from experience how puzzling events are in themselves and how much light can be thrown on them by prayerful meditation.

When were the apostles closer to Christ: when hearing words they did not understand, or when coming to understand words they could no longer hear? So, when were they best qualified to introduce us to their experience—which is also our own? I am not interested in what happened two thousand years ago unless it also throws light on what is happening today. I am no archaeologist: the Gospel would not hold my interest without its actuality. I see my life in the light of the Gospel, but I also read the Gospel in the light of my life. I have a direct contact with the evangelists, I share their experience. What they tell me helps me to understand my own experience more clearly, and my own experience helps me to understand their message. I find the Gospel passionately interesting because it is talking about me—and if you are shocked by such a declaration, just ask yourself if that isn't basically why anything interests you.

Scripture is revelation . . . of what happens in our lives. Try taking this as a guiding rule for interpreting the Scriptures: everything they tell happens in your life; everything that happens in your life is prophesied, lived in the Scriptures.

If the reporting of events there seems strange to your experience, be on your guard: you are reading it badly. The element of the "marvellous" in the Gospel is the enemy of faith—faith being the reading of the meaning of our lives—

all the angels, demons, and miracles, everything that leads you to think that God revealed himself then differently from the way he does now, that Jesus showed himself to his contemporaries in a different guise from the one in which he shows himself to you now. If you think this, your life will be devalued and emptied: God, for you, will be in a book, but not in your life. And if he is not in your life, he will never be in your prayer, because praying is taking note of God's presence, call, and plan in your life.

Of course, I would hesitate to believe on the basis of my experience alone, without the Gospel and Tradition, which do far more than just repeat it, to support it; they confirm and verify it through a host of witnesses. But I would not believe in the Gospel if I were unable to recognize it in my life. Christ lives with us every day; he has not left us orphans. He speaks, heals, forgives, performs transfigurations, multiplications of loaves, apparitions, resurrections. These are all daily events, happening now, in our time. Without seeing this, it is useless to believe in the Gospel.

To take some examples:

The Annunciation: do you believe in the Annunciation? Do not bother to answer—the question is of no interest. What should be asked—what you absolutely must ask yourself, in fact, is: "Have you had an annunciation? Tell us about your last annunciation." An annunciation is the account of a call, so give us an account of your calls—in your profession, your family, your marriage, your parenthood, your friendships, your parish. Have you been called? How, and how many times? The Catholic sickness: their faith in the Annunciation excuses them from experiencing any annunciations.

To be a little more definite, let us ask: "Have you seen an angel? How many times have you met angels? When was your last angel?" I am not asking if you believe in angels (if you do you'll find some lovely ones in fairy stories): I am asking about your experience of angels. What is an angel? Simply a messenger from God, someone who brings you an appeal, a mission, a light from God. In this sense, your life swarms with them. Religious education has the urgent task of helping us to recognize them by plucking their feathers, because if you believe angels have wings, two disastrous consequences will follow:

First—you will never see one (or if you do, you should go at once to the nearest good psychiatrist) and you will live a disinherited, profane life, one in which God never shows himself, never speaks, a life of "faith" in what happened two thousand years ago, of nostalgia for that wonderful time when the divine was within our grasp, a life lying in wait for everything that is most suspect in "religious" mentalities: visions, apparitions, miracles, stigmata, "prophecies," and infallible recipes for finding lost objects, obtaining "special favors," and getting out of desperate situations.

Second—you will think that it is God's fault that you have never seen one. There you are in the best of dispositions, asking nothing better than to see an angel; your whole life would be changed if only God would take the trouble to send you an angel. He used to send them all over the place; why is he so stingy with them now?

We always make the same mistake in prayer: we make God responsible for our own religious mediocrity and then invite him to change his ways. But the truth that we are always brought back to is that it is never God who needs to change, only us. If God had wanted to show himself through spectacular apparitions, that would mean that he had changed, that he had transformed himself to appear to us, and that there was therefore no need for us to *bother*. We could then go on waiting for a satisfactory revelation in our terms, whereas revelation always waits for us on terms that we can only grasp by really praying.

But in the New Testament, angels do not have wings—they wear white garments, that is, the usual form of clothing for that time and place. That means that today they wear sweaters and skirts, jackets and trousers, perhaps even Roman collars, since, after all, with God nothing is impossible. So the real question is: if the Blessed Virgin saw an angel (and note that St. Luke does not say that she did in so many words: he merely says she received—like any one of us—a message, a mission, a call from God), how did she recognize it? How did she know it was an angel?

The only possible answer is a striking one: in exactly the same way as we, in our lives, can recognize angels when we meet them. How do we know when a thought, a meeting, a happening comes from God? How do we know when we are called? It is a problem we often have to face up to in our lives, and it is exactly the same problem that Mary had to resolve for herself.

What did she do? Exactly what I hope we should do. First of all, the messenger made a good impression on her. When someone makes a good impression, particularly a religious impression, there are again two stupid courses we can take. One is to believe in it immediately. When faced with a religious impression, and above all with pious people, be careful: immediate belief is the road to all the worst sorts of illusion and credulity. The other is to reject it out of hand. So what is to be done? Use your good sense: nothing calls for it more than affairs of the supernatural. Faced with a religious call or impression, be patient, be watchful, check it, verify it.

Mary was a sensible girl. Her reaction was to wonder what the salutation meant and to ask: "How can this be?" She questioned, thought about, worked out the meaning of the whole of this extraordinary call. This must have taken time. A vocation does take time. Anything decided in two minutes is liable to last only two minutes. There is nothing in the account given by St. Luke to prevent us from believing that he has condensed a process that took several weeks, or even months, into a few dramatic moments. Later he tells us the secret of Mary's inner life: "They did not understand the saying which he spoke to them . . . and his mother kept all these things in her heart." So, at this most important moment in her life, she probably used the same process, and indeed Luke tells us that "she considered in her mind what sort of greeting this might be."

Then, she re-read the Scriptures. The words of the *Magnificat* show us that she sought to understand the meaning of what happened to her in her life in the light of the Prophets. And from them she learned that God always followed the same course of action in his dealings with his People: he chose young people rather than old, weak rather than strong, ordinary rather than great; and when he wanted a child for an extraordinary mission, the child was born to a barren woman. So it was perhaps not so strange that God had chosen her. If he wanted the poorest of the poor, perhaps she was just the person he needed.

Finally, she went and consulted someone experienced. Have you not often done the same when you have been called? She had heard that her cousin Elizabeth, as old as she herself was young for these matters, had had the same shock, the same grace. And what had Elizabeth done when she found herself pregnant in her old age? "For five months she hid herself"—in other words, she had gone away to give herself time, as so many of us would do when faced with a difficult call of this sort. For Mary, what had happened to Elizabeth was a sign, a confirmation, a way towards understanding of what was happening to her. And the Gospel tells that she "went with haste" to her cousin, unable to keep her secret to herself, to bear the burden by herself, any longer.

The two women who had been tested met and understood each other. They exchanged confidences, compared their experiences. And Elizabeth comforted Mary: "You are wonderful to believe like that; you are wonderful to dare believe that it came from God. In spite of my age and experience, I was absolutely shattered for five months, and I went and hid myself, so as not to think about it, not to hear anyone talking about it. But then I gradually pulled myself together, accepted it, understood that it was a chance, a favor, a blessing. And now I am so happy and proud. But your child is going to be a source of even greater joy than mine. Bless you for believing like that! Your faith is so much greater than mine. You are worth a thousand of me!"

And then Mary replied with her *Magnificat*. Not straight after her Annunciation: she was too overcome then. But after hearing her cousin it welled up out of her heart. This old woman who had suffered like her and who encouraged her in her faith was the real angel she met.

And how long does it take us to say our *Magnificat*? For our baptism, our vocation, our mission, our marriage, our celibacy? Three weeks? Three months? Three years? Thirty years? Mary spent three months rejoicing over her vocation. How long will we spend rejoicing over ours? Our lives too are full of God, full of annunciations, full of missions. Our lives too are peopled with angels, but as they are not feathered enough for our taste, we refuse to recognize them.

And what about transfigurations? How many times have we been at a Transfiguration? Which means: how many times has the Lord shown himself to you as never before, become close to you, alive for you in a way you would never have thought possible?

What happened at the Transfiguration?

For many Christians, the Gospel is a sort of mythology. In those days, they say, things happened that we are no longer worthy of, or that God has crossed off his list of generosities. For a few years, two thousand years ago, God emerged from his everlasting silence and showed himself properly—miracles, thunderbolts, thunder, luminous clouds, the lot. Now we are on our own again, with memories of the past and a longing for the Second Coming.

So for these Christians it has to be Christ who changed at the Transfiguration: as it is always God who is in the wrong, he has to meet the expense. So his face became shining like the sun, his garments white as snow; Moses appeared at his right hand and Elijah at his left, along with the inevitable cloud and voice from heaven.

But be careful: the evangelists often use commonplaces and symbolism in their language, and would be very surprised to find us taking them literally. Do you seriously think that God shows himself at a certain intensity of light? What voltage? It is not much use if Christ's face shines like the sun when the Hiroshima bomb can shine like a thousand suns. Or if his garments become white as snow when other brands wash whiter.

So what do God's "glory" and the "witness" of the Prophets consist of? If you pay attention only to the letter, you are soon inextricably in difficulty, and displaying a far more childish mentality than the "primitive" writers you affect to follow so faithfully; worse still, you are cutting yourself off from the world of God and from any chance of ever benefitting from a transfiguration.

In fact, as we know well, the hand of the Lord is still with us. The Word has become flesh, reality, revelation, for us too, and lives among us; we only have to change a little to realize this at last.

Christ was born once only because he is being born all the time.

Jesus spoke once only because he is talking to us all the time.

He suffered once from the incredulity and hard-heartedness of men only because he is suffering from them all the time.

And he was transfigured once only because he is constantly being transfigured for those who look on him with respect and love.

It depends on us. Only we have to change, always. We are the only obstacle in the way of the full manifestation of God.

In fact there was always a radiance emanating from the person of Christ, but the distracted and darkened vision of those around him failed to see it. Not all of them, for the Gospels tell how people "pressed about him" because of the power they sensed in him, and how he healed the sick. Do we not know people who have this sort of radiance about them? People who make us feel well when we are with them, who radiate friendship, joy, peace, and brotherly love? With them, too, there are people who cannot see this and even some who see it and mistrust it, so stay away for fear of being carried away.

Christ was in constant communication with his Father, he listened to him, consulted him. When people saw this, when they heard him talking about his Father, they said to themselves: "He knows what he is talking about. He's speaking from experience, not like the scribes and pharisees who repeat what others have told them. He speaks with authority, with real knowledge." And suddenly, in his presence, they discovered that we were made to have a Father, to believe in a Father, and yet we were behaving like orphans, like lost children. They could not hear the Son without being made spontaneously aware of their own calling as sons. But some did not listen and were aware of nothing.

And finally, Christ was in constant "dialogue" with the Scriptures. This is the real meaning of the appearance of Moses and Elias at the Transfiguration: Moses means the five books of the Law, and Elijah represents the Prophets. The Law and the Prophets together mean the whole of the Old Testament—remember Luke 24, 27: "And beginning with Moses and all the prophets . . ." Christ fulfilled the prophecies, so there was a dialogue, an exchange of "lights," between Christ and the Prophets. Christ's life was clarified in the light of the Scriptures, and the Scriptures could be better understood in the light of his life.

But the apostles, though they knew their Old Testament by heart, had never dreamt that it might be actual enough to come alive before their eyes. They set its events in a distant past or an indefinite future; they had never connected it with their own experience. A familiar enough approach, surely?

After their three years of "adult catechumenate," the apostles were still completely impervious to the divine. They had listened to innumerable sermons, and the more they heard, the less impression there was made on them. They were involved in "good works" up to their necks, and this did not seem to have made them visibly better. They witnessed astonishing events full of symbolism and meaning, but they looked for no more in them than the enhancement of their own importance.

Then Christ decided that they couldn't go on like that any longer. So he took them aside, away from the crowds they tried to order around. He took them on a retreat, in a calm and lonely place on a hillside. There, they calmed down, recollected themselves, shut up. They laid aside their cares and their ambitions, and so for once when they were alone with him they felt the full radiance of his presence, the intensity of his influence. They became attentive and began to hear him as they had never heard him before, to see him as he had always been in their midst, but as they had never noticed.

And suddenly they felt so happy that they wanted to stay there: "This is such a fine place. Wouldn't it be good to pitch our tents here!" They had not been too happy to come, now they were sorry it was so short. They had acquired a taste for retreats . . .

It is we who are responsible for transfigurations; God never refuses them; we just have to lend ourselves to them. Not only are we responsible for transfigurations, but also for disfigurations: think of all the closed, ungrateful, dimmed faces around us. Of all those who have failed to find a welcome, a smile, understanding, and whose light has gone out as a result.

So I am not asking if you believe in the Transfiguration: faith "in" the Transfiguration is liable to excuse you from experiencing transfiguration, and that sort of faith is really the opium of the people! I am not even asking if you have been at a transfiguration—one is not nearly enough. What I am asking is whether you have worked any transfigurations, whom you have transfigured.

Remember when you were engaged, in love, the joy you found in bringing a smile to your loved one's face, watching the expression on it transformed? How long now since you stopped transfiguring each other like that, how long since you stopped exercising your power of transfiguration over each other? Remember how, when your children were little, you never tired of attracting their attention, making them smile, filling them with confidence? Now their expressions are often closed and ungrateful and they sham indifference, but do you think you can still strip this mask off them, do you think you can still work your power of transfiguration on them?

Teachers of seriously sub-normal children have often told me of their amazement on seeing these usually blank, subhuman faces suddenly light up with a smile, a sign of understanding or a glimmer of achievement. There is nothing more beautiful than seeing someone's face light up—the face of an old man, a stranger, an outcast who suddenly finds himself treated with respect and love, who suddenly finds a friend. God shows himself in these faces. That is the Transfiguration: God, in all his glory, shows on the face of the stranger who for once has been welcomed, treated with consideration, cared for and loved. You will never have any other revelations of God than those you provoke, those you deserve in this way. But he who has once brought about and witnessed one of these revelations will know that nothing can be more divine; he will understand why God became man.

And what about multiplications of loaves—have you ever

been at any, lived any, worked any? I don't care if you believe in the multiplication of loaves: whether you do or not
is quite beside the point, irrelevant, an ideological game. I
am only interested in your experience.

I have seen multiplications of loaves. I have seen how
charity can spread, can multiply itself in an incredible way.
I have seen men multiply loaves.

For a long time, I must confess, the Gospel account was
just a miraculous story, which I could not assimilate to my
experience, and which therefore worried me. Then in 1966
the Little Brothers of the Poor invited me to preach their
annual retreat and told me about their beginnings. It all
began with one young man who had a heart: he learned
that two old men in his neighborhood were no longer capable of cooking for themselves, and refused to go into a
home. So he decided to take them a hot meal every day.
This he did for two years. People mocked him, pitied him,
or admired him, but it was a long time before anyone
thought of actually helping him. To them he said: "Better
if you go and look after others." Helpers multiplied; the
movement grew and spread. Today forty people give their
whole lives to it; hundreds of others—students, workmen,
farm laborers—give a year; thousands of others come and
help when they can, regularly, occasionally, in their holidays. They have given a new style to the care of the old.
Their motto is "Flowers before Bread," because they know
that what old people lack more than anything else is affection, and that those who feel useless and forgotten need to
be treated with special attention. They give a diamond ring
to couples celebrating their diamond wedding. A newspaper
found out that this ring was then buried with them, and
printed an indignant story. But that same evening someone
rang up and offered his chateau for the old people's holidays,
saying: "You have given poor people back their dignity."

Now do you understand what the multiplication of loaves
means?

What is so splendid about the Gospel account is that Christ did not just make bread—God did not do man's work for him. There had to be a young man (but then it is only the young who put themselves forward like this!) who had the temerity to suggest his five loaves and two fishes as food for five thousand. In other words there had to be someone willing to give up everything (who knows what price his loaves and fishes might have fetched on the black market?), a prudent ant among five thousand grasshoppers, prepared to commit himself, to take the risk, to start the ball rolling.

And from there it developed; generosity multiplied, became contagious. It is not only splitting atoms that starts a chain reaction. It happens in heroism, generosity, liberality as well. It is slow to start but quick to spread. Try it! How happy that young man must have been afterwards to see the magnificent results of his generosity!

Of course the story is too "marvellous," too much a changing of bread, not enough a changing of hearts. That is why it had a bad ending: they wanted to make him king, and Jesus had to run away and hide. The real miracle, to which no objection could be made, would be for Christ so to multiply our generosity as to obtain from each one of us the response he obtained from that young man, and for us to feed the world by pooling all our resources, obeying Christ's command:"*You* give them something to eat!" (Mark 6, 37).

In the desert, Christ refused to turn stones into bread; he refused to perform a spectacular but sterile miracle which required no collaboration from men. God respects man; he wanted to need men. God only shows himself as God through the intermediary of man. So we are responsible for multiplying loaves. If we do not do it, there will never be, and in a sense will never have been, any multiplications of loaves. Because it is impossible to believe that there have been and will be any, unless we know from experience that we, despite our inertia and egoism, are capable of performing them. And those who have seen loaves multiplied in this way, who have taken part in and worked the miracle, know that nothing could be more beautiful, more human and divine at once, and that God could not appear more God-like than through a man demonstrating the creative and inventive power of love.

And what about apparitions? When was your last apparition? Have there been many in your life? When did you last see the Lord? And when did you last fail to recognize him?

In the Gospel, the law of apparitions is very simple: no one recognizes Christ immediately when he meets him. This immediately involves us all, because we too are constantly meeting Christ without recognizing him. Christ is present in our lives: "I am with you all days . . ."; "I am at the door, knocking . . ."; "He who is of the truth hears my voice"; "The man who loves is born of God and knows God" (perhaps without recognizing him); "What you do to the least of my brethren . . ." But we fail to know him, just as the disciples did; Mary Magdalen thought he was the gardener; the disciples on the road to Emmaus thought he was just another traveller—a hitch-hiker or a tramp; at the miraculous draught of fishes, the apostles saw a stranger cooking bread and fish. A good enough selection of the sort of people we neglect every day.

He was anyone. The person who invented the image of Christ as "the most beautiful of the sons of man" would most deserve to be shot, if anyone in Christendom could. People like that cannot resign themselves—or rather raise themselves—to fidelity to the Incarnation. Christ, for them, has to be decked out somehow or other: if he cannot have wings then let us at least put a feather in his hat!

But the risen Christ not only did not look like God; he no longer looked like himself either. He was so anonymous that the disciples on the road to Emmaus walked several miles with him without recognizing him. Whom did he look like? Anyone! You. Me. If you want a vision of the risen Christ, look at your neighbor's face. That will give you the necessary shock of surprise to make you give up trying to recognize him by his face, his voice, his height. You will have to try a different approach: to accept the need to change if you are to see him changed, to give yourself a little if you are to receive him. You have to begin to look like him yourself to be able to recognize him.

We have met him in our lives. Perhaps you have known someone who did not inspire much sympathy in you to begin with, maybe because he was too dull, or even too brilliant . . . And then something happened to throw you together, and you began to talk to each other calmly and seriously. You started to see him under a new light; he told you things you would never have expected from him, perhaps even things no one had ever told you before, things that prompted you to say things you had never said before, had perhaps never even thought about. You would have liked the occasion to last forever: "Stay with us . . ." And then you might have said to yourself: "That was a real occasion in my life, an extraordinary moment; I've had a vision."

Were there ever any other sorts of visions? No, you have the same sort as the apostles had. And they were just as hesitant as you to recognize them for what they were.

He spoke to them as only he could. He forgave their cowardice, their desertion, as only God can forgive sins. He shared bread with them and served as he had done so often before. And they no longer dared to ask him: "Who are you?", because they knew perfectly well it was the Lord. Only he could wait on them like that; only he could talk to them like that; only he was so gay, so brotherly, so encouraging, so attentive that they never wanted to leave him, and yet felt ready to go on any mission he might have for them.

If we do not recognize our God in the same things, we shall never have any other apparitions. What more do we

want? Thunderclaps, phantasmagoria, signs in the heavens?
He became *man,* not thunder! If we will not see him in men,
do we think that we shall see him better in the elements?

We are all responsible for apparitions: do we treat our
neighbor with enough faith and respect to provide him with
an apparition—or are we so sulky that the mere sight of us
is enough to make any apparition go away? The family, the
classroom, friendships, are all settings that favor apparitions,
that bring out the best in us, where each one of us feels
encouraged, loved, trusted—where each one of us becomes
so much himself that he is no longer recognizable.

Our lives are full of God and we can pray all the time:
praying being taking stock of the fact that God is talking
to us, calling us, sending us. We can know that we re-live
the Gospel, that the real Gospel is our life, and that it begins today. And above all we can use our wonderful power
of transfiguration, of multiplication of loaves, of apparition,
of resurrection. St. Paul said: "If men are not risen, neither
is Christ risen." Which means: if you cannot see, feel, use a
power of resurrection, of liberation, in the world about you
today, then you have no right to believe in a Resurrection.

And the same goes for the multiplication of loaves: if men
today do not multiply their bread and share it out, what use
was it for Christ to have multiplied and shared out his so
long ago? And if men are not transfigured, if today we
do not recognize, with tenderness and fervor, the apparition
of God on the face of man, then for us there was never a
Transfiguration.

A setting for the continual manifestation of God in an
assembly of men—that is what a Church should be. "And
we all, with unveiled face, beholding the glory of the Lord,
are being changed into his likeness from one degree of glory
to another; for this comes from the Lord who is the Spirit"
(2 Corinthians 3, 18).

✧ V ✧

Prayer and Providence

What can we ask of God? Nothing!

We can ask nothing of God, I have said, because he has given us all he possesses. But what does he possess? What is his kingdom? What does he communicate to those who open themselves to him?

Nothing of what men think, for God is poor, God is weak, God is suffering, because he is only love. God can give nothing except giving, loving, becoming like him. Look at your crucified God: do you think you can try and wangle money, success, healing, favors ("a place at your right or left") out of *him*? What do you think the cross is: a lightning conductor? More likely to draw the lightning, exposed up there.

God tells us: "You are strong with my strength and joyous with my joy, for I have nothing else to give you." Christ did not die so that we should not die; he did not suffer so that we should not suffer; he died and suffered so that our death and suffering might be like his. You can only ask one thing of Christ crucified: to love and believe like him.

God's impotence resounds from Calvary. But pagan man ceaselessly reassures himself that God is only shamming weakness while really keeping his omnipotence—it is so much more comforting that way.

The idol we have to destroy is that of omnipotence. God

is not omnipotent; he can neither make a circle square nor take away man's freedom. Professing the omnipotence of God is denying the creation, denying freedom, making the Passion a pious comedy and bringing back Jupiter in the guise of Jesus Christ. And if God can prevent all the evil in the world, then he is responsible for it all.

God is not omnipotent in the way that we think—that is, in the way we should like to become omnipotent. He is omnipotence of love, not of force. How many of us worship a monster. We project our own desires on God: "If only I could do everything!" Well, what would you do? Do you honestly dare admit it? And is that what you think of God?

The real God is omnipotence of fatherhood, an all-powerful begetter, such a potent force of love that he is capable of raising up a son or daughter in each of us, a son or daughter who is like him. Fatherhood is the experience of total dependence, the experience of the unlimited power an infinitely fragile, infinitely dependent being has over you, of his omnipotence over your heart.

God could have been omnipotent if he had not been love, if he had had no one to love. He ceased to be when he created man and entrusted the world to him. By making man free, he deliberately limited himself. "I am free," said Gabriel Marcel, "to the extent that God limits his productive power." It is not we who limit God; it is God who created a being capable of resisting him, capable of introducing into the world elements that God did not wish. God created creators: a free act of ours cannot be foreseen, is not pre-contained in its antecedents; it brings in a new element. "In the course of evil, the creature is the first cause" (Maritain). That is, the creature is the creator.

In the Redemption, God wanted to have need of men. This does not contradict his power, but brings it out. In the same way, he could have created a world of robots, but how much more worthy of him that he should have preferred a world of free men with whom he would deal only in the freedom of love!

Christ is our Liberator in revealing the impotence of God: the pagan divinizes nature, and above all divinizes events, making them his masters (even Pascal, alas: "If God gave us masters from his hand, how wholeheartedly we should have to welcome them. Events are infallibly masters of this sort"), abandoning himself to "divine providence." Christ frees us from all this by showing us the true order in which God reveals himself to us: the order of love. God is not to be found in the appalling constraint that events put on us; he is to be found rather in the proposal he makes of his grace to enable us to rise above events. Paganism is resignation; Christianity is an initiative of freedom.

And the "religious" mentality still sees sure and adorable divine intervention in everything that happens. It kisses the hand that strikes as reverently as the hand that heals. It sacralizes the worst crimes by venerating the "will of God" in them—even Martin Luther King's poor widow: her first words, according to the newspapers, on learning of her husband's assassination, were: "God has willed it." A sorry sort of God! As soon as horror reaches a certain pitch, we instinctively divinize it—only God is big enough to be capable of such an atrocity! There is no attitude more deeply rooted in the hearts of the devout and all efforts to combat it are likely to be unavailing.

Let us try, however, because without a true understanding of providence it is impossible to arrive at a true practice of prayer. I should like to develop two propositions: everything does not come from God; nothing comes without him.

Everything Does Not Come From God

Fatalism is the great temptation of all religions. It is not only atheists who are determinists; the materialism that denies the freedom of man is strangely allied to the providentialism that sees "the hand of God" in everything. Many Christians are fatalists: "You have to bow down under the will of God . . . May his will be done . . . It's fate . . . It is written . . . It had to happen . . ."

Do you think the hand of God sends us events to be our masters? Do we have to accept them in self-abandonment to divine providence, or react against them by appealing to our creative resources? If someone knocks on your door, is he automatically sent by providence? No, you know that refusing to let him in can be just as "providential" as letting him in. Let us try to live up to our responsibilities!

Providentialism leads straight to atheism: "Man becomes atheist when he is better than the God he serves." If God does good, then he is responsible for evil. If he protects and spares you, then he sacrifices your neighbor. After the Liberation in the Second World War the Franciscans in my neighbourhood held a special service of thanksgiving because God had spared their convent in an Allied bombardment. It was only the houses round about that were destroyed!

"If God permits the suffering of a single child, when he could prevent it, then I am an atheist" (Robinson). No, man must not abandon himself to providence; it is God who abandons himself to man, God who abandoned the government of the world to the laws he established and the freedom he created. It is false to say that God controls the world, constantly loading the dice we throw. God respects the liberty of his creatures. You cannot understand the world if you seek to find the reflection of God's will in it, but it all becomes clear if you see the consequences of man's will in it.

God does not wish evil and it would be blasphemous to believe that he did. Neither does he allow evil, as we tend too often to say, as a sort of half-measure trying to defend God's responsibility and his power at once. A God who permits evil, a God indifferent or insensible to evil, is not the

God of Jesus Christ. No, God does not permit evil; he is against it! He fights against it with all the means at his disposal, inspiring those who struggle against it. He suffers from our evil: he could not bear to see us suffer and die, so he came to suffer and die to deliver us from evil by showing us a love capable of overcoming all evil. God recognizes himself in all who hunger and thirst after justice, all who take up arms against evil, not in those who "permit" evil in a spirit of prudent neutrality.

But his weapon is love: this is his only strength, and to us it seems like weakness. Evil is strong, admired, rich, organized, powerful. God is like a child on the battlefield of the world, fighting against evil with empty hands and bare head, without hatred or violence, often alone against the rest, but continuing to believe in his ultimate victory: "When I have been lifted up, I will draw all things to me."

No, God does not send us suffering, sickness, and death; they are not trials, penances, or examinations—God as schoolmaster is as unattractive as God as executioner.

"But," you may ask, "surely parents punish children for their own good, out of love?" Maybe, but God does not treat us like children; he treats us like adults, as free men. If he had kept any power over us, he would not have "loved us to the end."

Suffering and sickness: the old Jewish idea of temporal retribution is still alive in all religions: misfortune is guilt; God rewards the good and punishes the wicked. The Anglican *Book of Common Prayer* comforts the sick with a prayer beginning: "Whatever the illness, know first that it is sent by God"!

Of course the punishment can be softened from time to time by calling it a "test," or by insinuating that God sent it for our sanctification—but this is still God as *deux ex machina*, the all-purpose excuse for not thinking or acting, the God of resignation. You cannot go into a religious-run hospital without some sister or almoner explaining away the providential meaning of your illness or accident!

Why don't they read the Gospel? On every page Christ is healing the sick, but who could imagine he made them sick? God revealed himself as consoler, and we make him afflicter.

Death: this is the subject *par excellence* for bringing out our deep, indelible paganism. Christ did not kill anyone; the true God is "lord over death." Christ raises from the dead, gives the son back to his mother, the brother back to his sisters, the daughter back to her father—and yet all Christians believe that he "delights" in separating them! God is the greatest of murderers. On memorial cards you can read: "It has pleased the Lord to call his servant . . ." What a sadist! It has pleased him, it has been his good pleasure, to take a child away from its mother or a husband away from his wife?

But Christ wept over the death of Lazarus; he was moved with pity for the grief of the widow of Nain; he begged "with great cries and tears" not to have to die. And Christians believe that he kills them off at will, when he wants, where he wants, as he pleases.

I have had widows tell me that they have lost their faith when their husbands died, not because of their own sufferings, but because of the "Christian" consolations. They had just had enough of hearing: "God has called your husband back to him. God has taken your husband. God is testing you. God always punishes those he loves. You're lucky, really." And who can blame them?

Things like this, which may once have been consoling, revolt us today because man has become conscious of his freedom and no longer tolerates a despotic and bloodthirsty God. But God does not kill; he raises from the dead. God is not the one who has taken your husband or your child; God is the one who will give him back to you. Don't cut yourself off from the one who is going to reunite you.

"Death was never of God's fashioning; nor for his pleasure does life cease to be," says the Book of Wisdom (1, 13). What killed your husband or your child is the disorder, the wickedness, the sin of the world. We have not researched enough, worked enough, struggled enough; God entrusted his creation to us with sufficient resources to overcome evil and repair the ravages of sin. If as much money and as much scientific effort were put into cancer research as into chemical and biological warfare, don't you think we would have found a cure by now?

Whatever the outcome, research would be a better approach than "bowing down before the mighty hand of God." If it were God's will that man should die, then it would be sacrilegious to oppose it. But we believe that it is God's will that man should live, and so it is our sacred duty to fight against death.

In the Canadian marriage rite the bride and groom make their vows "for as long as it shall please God to keep us together." Here again is the old pagan god taking his pleasure among men; one moment he is pleased to unite you, and the next he is pleased to tear you apart. Nemesis, the goddess who was jealous of human happiness, is easily reintroduced into the Christian mentality. A very devout widow once said to me: "We were too happy, you know, it couldn't last"; and a mother who had just lost a child: "We have to pay for our happiness." Such is the God they imagine: nothing is for nothing; you just keep paying; you pay on your way in, you pay on your way out and don't forget the Guide!

"The Lord has given, the Lord has taken away, blessed be the name of the Lord," said a wonderful—but providentialist—mother. But no, Mrs. L., the Lord did not give you your child: you know how babies are born. It certainly isn't providence that sends them: don't try to evade your responsibilities! And it was no more the Lord who took it away than it was the Lord who gave it to you: your child died from a well-determined or determinable disease, which we shall find a cure for when we are all more united and more loving.

The discovery of secondary causes and knowledge of the laws of nature have pushed Jupiter out of the territory he was usurping, but do no damage to the true God, who operates on another plane—that of grace.

Remember the interpretation that was long put on Christ's sad statement: "The poor you have always with you." It was taken as indicating that the order "willed by God" required that there should always be rich and poor. And don't forget that you will resemble the God you imagine: do you want to be a God who sends trials, war, famine—a God who allows evil? Better, surely, the God who could not bear to watch humanity suffer and took humanity upon himself so that he could share the struggle with us?

But people still cling to their ways; they are attached to their superstitions: God is such a convenient explanation and his attentions, even if they bring trouble, are flattering. Tell someone who is seriously ill or has had an accident that his troubles are simply due to chance (that no one could have foreseen them or wished them on him), and he will be far more offended than if you blame God for them. At least, with God, they mean something.

How does one answer this? It is not so bad when one thinks only of the recipient. But think for a moment of the role you are assigning to the sender. Imagine yourself as a father passing on a serious infection to your child "for his own good," to make him think! No? Well, God does not behave like that either. Read the Gospel. But this does not mean that your illness has no meaning: the fact that its origin is not divine does not mean that it cannot be put to divine use. Illnesses can be put to good use; there is a grace of healing or of rising above offered to every invalid. God is Redeemer: is that not enough for you? Does he have to be Avenger as well?

But the objection bounces back: "Nevertheless, the Bible

tells of divine punishments; God punished Adam and Eve."

No, God punishes no one. God judges no one. God damns no one. Man judges himself ("Men have preferred the darkness to the Light"), man punishes himself, damns himself. God's intervention is always an intervention of love: a warning, a suggestion, a pardon. If, in the Genesis story, you take God's "commandment" as a threat—"If you eat that fruit, I'll kill you"—you succeed in becoming atheist of (that is, better than) that God. Would you tell you child: "If you steal that lump of sugar, I'll kill you"? It has to be taken rather as a solicitous warning: "Don't do that. It won't be good for you. You're not mature enough for it. That way leads to death." If you neglect that warning, and find yourself ill as a result, can you say: "God has punished me"? How unfair: he did everything he could to save you from it.

But—again—the Gospel says: "Not a hair falls from your head without . . . your Father who is in heaven."

A formula often used to express the workings of providence, this is obvious to primitive peoples who hardly distinguish between first and second causes, but it is no longer obvious in our more sophisticated civilization. The same truth has to be expressed in function of a new mentality. So what do we put in after that "without"? If it is "the will of," then God is a sadist who tears your hair out. "The permission of," then? Then God is an indifferent and superior spectator casually accepting your physical decline. But if it is "the attention of," then it just means that God is interested, takes it to heart, gives you grace to rise above it, overcome it, be happier bald than you were hairy!

Jesus often spoke of providence in terms that strike us as naïve, optimistic, and superficial, because he was using the conventions of the popular speech of his day: "God clothes the lilies of the fields, feeds the birds (often very badly!); he makes his sun rise (often causing drought and famine), and his rain fall (in floods sometimes)." The problem is simple: Jesus was not distinguishing between first and second causes; like the folk wisdom of even our time, he attributes everything globally to God. His message was expressed in a way comprehensible to the mentality of his age. We have to keep the message, but not the form in which it is wrapped. And the message here is clear enough: "Don't worry." Christ here is not warning us against work, but against worry; not against occupation, but against preoccupation; not against action, but against agitation—"Martha, you are troubled about many things . . ."

To sum up: the old pagan religion regarded God as the Master of the universe, the maid of all work and the all-purpose explanation of creation. This belief is so natural to the human mind, so instinctive, that it has never been totally eradicated by Christianity—which has, indeed, sometimes abetted it as producing "religious" attitudes. At present, in our scientific, technological age, this attitude makes people atheist. Man has become lord of the world; he judges it and improves it. He can no longer believe in a God who exists on the "natural" plane—a God, that is, of power, fear, and self-interest. He has now become ripe for the revelation of Christ; he can believe in a God who exists on the plane of love. The atheist who rejects a God who brings oppression, fear, suffering, and tyranny is infinitely more Christian, in any real sense, than the Christian who is still happy with this sort of God.

While man was still weak and defenceless in the face of epidemic, famine, winter, and darkness, he bowed his head in humble adoration of the God who sent all these scourges. He kissed the hand that struck him down and the hand that fed him: these were one and the same—the hand of Nature. But Revelation has liberated man by desacralizing nature. God says: "Dominate nature and make it subject to you. I have only one excuse for making such a harsh, hostile, and inhospitable world for you to live in, and that is to have made you, man, a creator, capable of improving and finishing off my work. I am not proud of the world as it

came from my hands, but I will find my justification in the
completion you bring to it. You are not a slave whose duty
is to thank me and respect my work; you are my son, you
take charge, you work with me, and you take the responsibility and the initiative."

2. Nothing Happens Without God

Clearly, we are not denying God any intervention in the
world: we are only doubting that his interventions are vio-
lent. All religious people believe that God has a care for
them. But before the scientific era, men looked for proof of
this care on the level of "phenomena," in acts of power in
which God would show himself and impose himself. The
scientific mode of thought makes us more and more allergic
to this outlook.

We believe that God intervenes without cease, but in
keeping with his nature as revealed in Jesus Christ, respecting the laws he has established and the liberty with which
he has endowed us. God intervenes in the psychological and
moral order; he talks to us, calls us, proposes himself to us,
but imposes himself never. We live in an order of grace,
which is of freedom, not of subjection. God constantly
shows himself, but by signs of love, not acts of power.

If everything does not come from God, nothing happens
without him. All the things that he never wished—suffering,
sin, and death—he proposes a remedy for. He continually
inspires, in us and in others, a love capable of overcoming
or remedying evil. But he only shows himself as God
through the intermediary of man.

There is a meaning in, a use to be made of, a way to be
found out of, every circumstance of our lives. God does not
bring events; he suggests how we might use them in order
to free ourselves from their domination. He does not prevent
disasters; he is with us in them. He offers us the grace to
be happier poor than we would have been rich, to be happier

in sickness than we would have been in health, happier when we are persecuted than when we are flattered, happier in misfortune than when everything is going well.

Christ did not come down from the cross, so let us not ask him to do so now, but that we on our cross may be like him—loving, faithful, attentive to others and still active. He carried on his apostolate on the cross. He converted people from the cross. Your cross may strip you of authority, prestige, riches, or strength; it does not strip you of love. "When I have been lifted up, I will draw all things to me."

This is the view of providence that St. Paul expounds in Romans 8, 28–39. "We know that in everything God works for good with those who love him, who are called according to his purpose. For those whom he foreknew he also predestined to be conformed to the image of his Son, in order that he might be the first-born among many brethren . . . What then shall we say to this? If God is for us, who is against us? He who did not spare his own Son, but gave him up for us all, will he not also give us all things with him? . . . Who shall separate us from the love of Christ? Shall tribulation, or distress, or persecution, or famine, or nakedness, or peril, or sword? . . . No, in all these things we are more than conquerors through him who loved us. For I am sure that neither death, nor life, nor angels, nor principalities, nor things present, nor things to come, nor powers, nor height, nor depth, nor anything else in all creation, will be able to separate us from the love of God in Christ Jesus our Lord."

VI

Prayer and Action

Christianity recognizes no distinction between prayer and action.

"There is a certain class of demons that can only be chased away by prayer"—the demons of deafness to God, dumbness in thanksgiving, self-sufficiency, worry, despair and solitude. But there is another class that can only be chased away by action—the demons of illusion, sentimentality and infantilism, narcissism and laziness. So if we cultivate prayer exclusively, we harbor the second lot, and if we cultivate action exclusively, we harbor the first lot.

Christianity leaves the famous and false distinction between action and contemplation far behind: it is participation; its prayer is love in action and its action is inspired by love. God is not the object and fixed goal of our quest; he is its active principle, cause and motive power. Love is not made to be loved, but to be loving.

Pagan contemplation is a striving of man towards God (for a definition: "The sum total of techniques employed to experience direct contact with God"); Christian prayer is infused into man under the action of the Holy Spirit: it is God striving towards man. God prays in us as he loves in us; praying is lending ourselves to him enough for him to take total possession of us. Once he has come alive in us, he does in us what he loves doing himself: he forces us in the direction of others. God is far more pleased with us when we are loving others than when we are loving him; in the first case, he can recognize himself in us, know that he has taken us over completely: "All that is his is ours," our life has become as God-like as our prayer; we have a "share" in him. "Believing," as Father Manaranche has said, "is accepting love to be able to love."

Division of labor into manual and cerebral has already had a sufficiently dehumanizing effect for us not to seek to extend it into the domain of piety. Why tear Christ in half? He worked and prayed: would we try to be better than him? If all that was needed to save the world was hymns and "intentions," there would have been no need for Christ to become man; he could have stayed in the perfect monastery of heaven, a "cloistered paradise" with an inviolable grille.

The Christian will never devote himself exclusively either to prayer or to action; he will only place differing emphases on one or the other in his life. In our spiritual journey, the starting point does not matter much: the important thing is where we arrive. At the outset, one's choice of an active or contemplative life is decided mainly by one's natural inclinations; it is a question of temperament. The only supernatural qualification is the end of the road: will the contemplative have been led to action, to charity; will the man of action have been led to prayer?

The greatest contemplatives have been outstanding men of action, which is understandable: they have contemplated so well, become so impregnated with the "saving God," the God who "works without cease" and who died working on the Cross, that they have come to resemble the God they have contemplated. For the only object of Christian contemplation is the humanity of Christ: "No one has seen God; it is the only Son who is in the bosom of the Father who has revealed him to us." And every true man of action has realized that he had to give men far more than his love and the revelation of God's love for us, far more than his face and his transfiguration, far more than his riches and what God could do in his poverty and that of others; he had to efface himself in prayer and action, die to his own desires and ambitions and rise again to the desire, devotion and unconditional love of Christ.

So both will have been led "where they did not wish to go" (John 21, 18). Their prayer will have become their life and their life their prayer. Christian mysticism flourishes in charity. Louis Bouyer, in his *The Meaning of the Monastic Life*, says that even the form of monastic life farthest removed from the world only finds its fulfillment in spiritual paternity. Prophetism (of the Christian variety) is opposed to mysticism (of the pagan variety): it proclaims that God has a *plan* to be carried out, that there is social justice to be achieved. It is therefore resolutely active, but it springs from inspiration, it proceeds from intimate contact with God, and its end is not "the sweet leisure of contemplation," but the benefits this can bring to others.

Prayer should make a prophet of each one of us. Praying is reminding ourselves of God's plan for the salvation of the world and his appeal for our collaboration in it. It is not a peaceful intimacy with the Lord (Jesus and me heart to heart) but participating in his work of Redemption. How could a God who "works without cease" be content with static adoration? God does not ask us to contemplate him, but to be like him.

Here we must praise St. Ignatius for his revolutionary initiative in founding an active Order and daring to suppress the Choir Office, the basis and center of all monastic life in the Middle Ages. He saw that God did not want people who "thought about" him, but men to do his will, not everyone who cries (or sings) "Lord, Lord," but those who work with him.

Do you know what contemplatives are like? The first time I went into a Trappist monastery I expected to find them all with their eyes raised to heaven, liable at any moment to ecstasy and levitation. But what I learned to admire was their realism. A true contemplative is someone lucid enough to perceive God where he really is: in his brothers. And it needs a very sharp eye and long practice in contemplation to see God in every one of our neighbors! A Christian monastery is one where the inmates love one another, where God's presence becomes visible and tangible because there are several gathered together there in his name.

A Cistercian friend of mine came back from a visit to a Trappist monastery in Africa full of enthusiasm: "I've found out, at last, what a monastery is for," he said.

"My dear Father, it's taken you some time . . ."

"Listen, it's splendid: down there, the whole countryside for a hundred miles round lives on the monastery. People come there to learn agriculture, reading, sewing, metalwork, nursing—and how to pray. And don't think this stops the monks from praying! Not at all, they feel themselves to be the soul of religion, with real spiritual responsibility for it; they've got something to pray about."

"Here," he added, "we're in a rut, we're not teaching anybody anything."

The monks of the West created the civilization of Europe for centuries; they did here what they are now doing in the Third World. Why did they not go on with their work here? What turned them from being the pioneers of civilization into its museum attendants and archaeologists? It has nothing to do with their contemplative vocation—it can only be that they have become less faithful to it.

During the retreats of the Lay Fraternities of Charles de Foucauld, the Blessed Sacrament is exposed for six days, with a continual rota of watchers. But on the last day, I always make this little speech: "You have venerated the sacrament as the permanent presence among us of God's gesture of love offering and service. And I hope you have meditated on it enough to be filled with it.

"Now I am going to break this Host into as many fragments as possible, and give it to you in communion at our last Mass. Has your meditation been sincere and deep enough for you to follow the Host into its new dwelling place? The Host does not want to stay in the monstrance; Christ has only one desire: to come into your brothers. Will your love and respect follow him there? It was easy enough to adore him while he was stuck up there, silent and harmless, but will you still adore him when he is made flesh in your wife or your husband, your children, your relatives, your neighbors?

"Christ hates the gold and silver in which he is usually imprisoned; he likes living in sinners, and only God knows if you are all sinners enough to give others the chance of respecting him in you."

Prayer divorced from action degrades man just as it disfigures God (see our remarks on providentialism). The effects of a prayer that tries to palm off on to God what we should be doing ourselves are thoughtlessness and the abdication of personal responsibility.

In Canada, I once had this "revelation" from a paralyzed man: "I have been ill since I was six. My parents were as Christian as people are in the villages round here, and for years they took me on pilgrimages, once or twice a month. Only God could cure me, only a miracle could save me, they said. Just think what my life was like: every time there was a wild hope, then the wait, then the disappointment, then the journey back. And once we got home, they started planning the next pilgrimage."

For years this boy was excused from coming to terms with his illness, prevented from becoming a man.

"When I was nearly sixteen," he went on, "I couldn't stand it any more; I rebelled against my parents and against God. I didn't want to hear any more about faith, prayer, or religion. I began to study hard, I really worked, I got a diploma and now I have a job. Now I'm thirty-five, I've looked at the religious thing again, and I've found faith again—but not the faith that kept me a child; a man's faith this time."

Whatever you ask from God, God can only ask you to do.

Whatever you receive from God, God has only you to pass on to others, because only you can make them receptive to his gifts if they refuse them.

If prayer does not grow up, there is no end to its mystifications. If someone says: "I'll pray for you," you can be quite sure that will be the last thing he will do for you, that he considers you a hopeless case which he is going to place "in God's hands." Unfortunately, ours are the only hands God has.

The old French grace before meals asked: "Bless us, Lord, bless this meal, bless this welcoming table . . . and give bread to those who have none! So be it!" In other words: "I'm sitting down to my meal. I'm looking after myself. Lord, you look after the rest!" Each for himself and God for all!

The "welcoming table" was gradually replaced by "those who have prepared it"; now an effort is being made to Christianize "give bread to those who have none" by substituting "make us find bread for those who have none." I should prefer: "You have shared your bread so well with us that you have given us the desire, and sometimes even the courage, to share our bread with others." The "so be it" would still have to be replaced by a less feeble, less "begging," translation of "Amen": "That's right; we'll do it; we want to."

How difficult it is to formulate a Christian prayer.

But modern man rebels against the hypocrisy of loading God with the tasks that we ought to perform ourselves. Unless a new way of praying is found for him, he will no longer pray at all. Surely it's only a pagan survival to pray

for rain or fine weather? Do you really think God decides
the temperature? If he does, what is he going to think when
man controls the weather, as one day he undoubtedly will?

Conversation between a parish priest and a seven-year-old
boy:

Priest: "It is God who makes the sun shine and the rain
fall."

Boy: "No, it's Daddy."

Priest: "What do you mean?"

Boy: "He looks after the crops, and when it looks like hail,
he seeds the clouds and makes them rain instead."

This rainmaker God is in permanent retreat before human progress. We too often try to give our children faith
with arguments that will make them atheists by the time
they are sixteen. Another example: in a mountain village
always short of water the whole population religiously
turned out on rogation days to pray for rain. The local
authorities sent some engineers who built a dam, the vil-
lagers now have a constant water supply and have given
up going on processions. Irrigation has replaced rogation.

There is another moral to this story, besides the obvious
one: it is just as bad for the organizers of the irrigation to
take no part in "rogation" as it is for the organizers of the
rogations not to be those who undertook the irrigation.
When those who pray don't work, those who work stop
praying. Praying is no excuse for not working, and work
is no excuse for not praying.

Prayer (one can never say it too often) is not a question
of getting out of God the things he would not otherwise
have given us. When I was studying Thomist philosophy,
prayer was explained by: "Of course man cannot change
God or modify the eternal laws. But God has decided from
all eternity only to accord his grace to those who pray.
Posita causa, sequitur effectus." Which being freely ren-
dered means: God holds out a lump of sugar to man and
says: "Good dog? Here's some sugar then." But one had to

have been a good dog for quite some time, because such are God's "rights."

No, prayer is not like that; prayer is opening oneself to God soliciting us so that he can communicate his energy, his creative, loving joy to us. From all eternity, God has given up his "rights" and given his creature unlimited power: everything we really ask for will be given to us, we shall hold on to everything we really love, be filled to overflowing with everything we really open ourselves up to, as with that "living water that becomes a gushing fountain in the heart of the man who believes."

A naïve but widespread idea of prayer: man prays for a favor, his prayer goes up to God, who works a sort of bank system in heaven, makes the necessary credit transfers, and the credit comes down on the head of the favor payee.

The real scheme of things is quite different: it is not you, then God, then the other. It is God "knocking at your door," besieging you with all the pity and love he feels for the world, then you, a lock-keeper who decides to let this flood of love through or not, and then the other you pass it on to, or not. *You* are the one who decides, your power of inter- cession, and intervention, surpasses anything you can imag- ine: "If you had faith, you could move mountains," not: "If you had faith, God would put the mountains where you asked him to."

You are the one who has the power; it is not you who have to go through God to get what you want, but God who has to go through you to get what he wants. Grace cannot reach others unless you let yourself become a channel for it; you will not change the world unless you yourself are changed first. Work out the price of your prayer: God will not be God except through you; God will not save the world without you.

The old conception was certainly more convenient: only God had to change; we could stay the same. For the price of a few "pious practices," we could buy exemption from the draft of world-savers.

The great religious mystification: prayer alone, pure prayer exempts us from action. No, there is nothing purely spiritual in the Church. The Church operates on a level neither materialistic nor idealistic, but on the sacramental level, which means that grace comes through outward signs, by becoming flesh, through men, not through all those "good intentions" that pave the road to hell. This is why those contemplative orders who are apparently devoted to "pure prayer" prefer to set up new houses in mission countries. Theoretically, they could pray just as well, if not better, without the bother and expense of the move. But they feel the instinctive urge to be a sacrament, an outward sign of God's love for men who do not know him.

Whenever you "pray for" someone, the first effect of your prayer should be to make you go out and look for something you can do for him. And once you take this view, you discover this truth—that there is always something to do. But the faithful who do not think will never believe it.

Go and prospect that whole enormous region left lying fallow by the mystification of prayer. The first reaction to what I have just said is always the same: "Yes, but there are always people one can't do anything for." And I have known worthy Christians add: "In Vietnam, for example." Can't one? Think hard: what movement have you taken the trouble to find out about, subscribed to (and lapsed!), worked for, demonstrated with, sent out information about, collected signatures and money for? Have you written to your local government representative? The tiniest pebble thrown into a lake will make ripples spread right across it!

I am sure there must be visible signs to transmit grace: only the love of Christians will convince men of God's love for them. Only the Church's sharing of its bread will convince men of the existence of God's bread. If every one of your prayers had led to some action: writing a letter, sending a book, making a telephone call, speaking up for someone, informing yourself better about something, getting in touch with X or Y, the face of the world would be changed.

Prayer is opening ourselves to God so that he can open us to others.

Have you noticed the real reproach addressed to the pharisee in the Temple? He gave thanks, certainly, but while he gave thanks for his fasting he was failing to see the greater opportunity for giving thanks offered in the person of the publican on whom he could have taken pity. By refusing to recognize his resistance to God, he failed to feel God's pity for him, and so felt no pity for the sinner: in failing to open himself to God, he failed to open himself to others.

True love is seen in action, shows itself in engagement. But this can also be in the mind, because I am sure that a sincerely loving thought about someone is immediately effective. Praying is also "thinking lovingly about someone." Love creates a "communion of saints," an immediate channel of communication between those it unites. As soon as you think lovingly of someone, I am sure you can influence him. And if the physicists and biologists can find some "sensory waves" to lend support to this love, so much the better.

But this must not be taken as denying the need for action: if sincere love acts on its own the moment it comes into existence, it would obviously not go on being sincere if it rested on the laurels of its existence to excuse it from commitment. If it did, it would soon cease to have any sort of influence.

The statement that "prayer is the soul of every apostolate" needs challenging. First of all, prayer is just as active as action, once you admit that there is nothing more active than profound receptiveness. Secondly, action is just as God-directed, just as receptive as prayer. The soul of the apostolate is none other than the soul of prayer: participation in the manner of God's love for man.

It was the fashion for a long time to claim that union with God only came through prayer and the sacraments; outside them, one could only try to remain at the level of sanctity that one had already reached. The Christian life was seen as an alternation between moments when one "recharged one's batteries" (retreats, pious practices), and times when one let them run down.

Action, in fact, is as sanctifying as prayer if it is as inspired. Modern spirituality has to take account of the fact that men now have less and less time to devote to "prayer" and cannot pray at set times. We absolutely must have a "spirituality of action" if we are to learn to "pray ceaselessly." If you must talk, wait a second and consult the Holy Spirit; be like someone receiving a visit or listening; without your knowing it, grace will be your guide. When you are questioned, swallow your reply and wait a second to hear what you should say; it is particularly when you talk that you must know how to listen. If you are going to see someone, pause for a moment, so that you can take Another with you.

Your inspirations will be measured by your aspirations.

"That's all very well," you may object, "but I can think of lots of people who claim they pray all the time, with the result that they virtually never do at all."

"Are they more numerous," I would ask in reply, "than the protagonists of 'pious exercises' who, once they are tired of their methods, take virtually no sort of exercise at all?"

But I am absolutely not claiming that you do not have to exercise yourself from time to time in order to pray all the time. Praying is looking at the map, and the farther you travel, the more you have to consult the map. Obviously your aim is the destination, but you won't get there without the map. And yet you will so often hear people say, "I love travelling so much and I have to do such a lot of it that I never have time to look at the map." That's no way to go far!

What does looking at the map mean? It means recognizing your starting point and your destination. If you want to pray, just ask yourself these questions: Who sends you? Who is leading you? Who inspires you, feeds you, gives you life and brings you back to life? Do people who see you see the Father who sent you, or just your gloomy, mean face? And where are you going? What do you look for in people you meet, what does your passing through do for people? Have you faith enough to see the God hidden in everyone, waiting to be loved so that he can grow in everyone? Did you come from God and are you going to God? Jesus knew that the Father had put all things in his hands, that he came from God and that he was going to God . . .

What does one do when one has come from God and is going to God? Do what he did: take a towel, wrap it round you and start to wash their feet . . .

This is where prayer and action meet; when you are full of God, penetrated by him, inspired by him, you go to the cross like him, which means you go to work like he did, you wash people's feet, or clean their shoes, or cook for them—you do the equivalent of what he did: you help others.

People ask, "How often, then, should you look at the map every day?" There's no answer to this sort of question; it all depends on the sort of journey you're making. If you are on a freeway (sometimes God is present all the time) there is no need to stop. But when you get into the side roads you constantly have to check that you are going the right way. And sometimes you feel completely lost: it might take a good half-hour poring over the map then to find out where you have got to. Then where would you have been without the map?

Studying the lives of the saints, I find they spent hours looking at the map in the early stages of their journey, and travel long distances without having to consult it in the later stages. Don't start where they finished; you may find yourself going round in circles.

Praying is listening to the sort of noise we make when the Word of God strikes us. What a weak, confused, muffled sound it is. We must go and practice, with the tuning-fork of the Holy Spirit, how to give out a sound that is clear and in pitch, go away and tune our instrument, then come back into the concert. Then people will really be pleased to listen to us.

VII

Let's Demythologize the
"Our Father"

Prayer is not reciting formulas.

Prayer is not reciting formulas, but welcoming inspiration. Nothing teaches us how to forget how to pray quicker than "saying prayers." No one can pray without consulting the creative Spirit, just as no one can talk without knowing how to listen. It's a case of waiting patiently till we become capable of hearing him. Just as water becomes transparent when it is still, so we will see most clearly when we are calm. The most peaceful waters move obediently at the least breath of wind.

Like every sacrament and the whole of the Christian life, prayer is a participation in the death and resurrection of Christ. We have to die to our will, ideas and impulses, and rise again to God's will, his plan of salvation, his patience of love. It takes a long time and it hurts to die; it takes a long time and hurts to come to life again. Christ spent a whole night saying one of the requests of the "Our Father": "not my will but thine be done," and we rattle the whole thing off in a few seconds! This is to say it without dying and rising again in the Spirit, it is making a pagan prayer under a Christian veneer, and this is what we are saying:

"Our Father, stay in heaven; don't bother too much with us; don't interfere in our affairs. As long as I am in control,

I'm happy, but as soon as you take over, God knows where you will drive us.

"My name be honored, known and esteemed, or at least the name of my family or community.

"My kingdom come, may my influence spread, my possessions increase.

"And, above all, may my will be done, because why should I want anything else?

"My bread is safe in my wallet, in my cellar, in my refrigerator. If perchance, Lord, you were to spread a little jam on my bread, I would be amazed, but it wouldn't come amiss. But for essentials, of course, I rely on myself; one has to be careful about important matters.

"I forgive so that I may buy and merit your pardon.

"Do not send us too many trials and disasters, but deliver us from our enemies. Amen!"

That's quickly said, but to say it properly, in the way the Spirit of Christ prompts us to, takes a long time. But let us try to learn: the task is an urgent one—discovering a prayer for modern man, learning an "Our Father" that Christ would teach us today: the same and yet so different that we should hardly recognize it—just as his contemporaries could hardly recognize what they had always been taught in his teachings. This is the essential task for evangelization today: to find out how Christ would have preached the Gospel today—quite differently from two thousand years ago, and yet the same Gospel!

And we are constantly told: "The 'Our Father' is the most sacred thing we have, the prayer we have clung to most." Yet, as Blondel wrote in his letter on the demands of contemporary thought: "To think today literally as we did five hundred years ago inevitably means thinking in a different spirit." Alas, it is not five hundred, but two thousand years that we have spent repeating the "Our Father" without "translating" it, except for the awful literalism of the reintroduction of "Lead us not into temptation"!

The result of this? I would be willing to bet that not a single boy or girl today can say the "Our Father" with any joy the way we teach it. The phraseology as it stands is mystifying and alienating; it teaches error about God and about us; it needs a mental correction making to each line. We believe as we pray; the first prayer we teach our children will determine their idea of God. And the damage that can be done by a misguided early religious education is ineradicable.

For a start: FATHER!

Does religion lead to infantilism? Aren't we Christians condemned, or authorized, to remain children all our lives because we have a Father, and an almighty one at that? His knowledge makes up for our ignorance, his strength for our weakness. We can remain little, ignorant, and passive because we trust in "him who knows better than we," "without whom we can do nothing." If man enhances himself, God humbles him. But if he humbles himself, God will raise him up.

Of course the problem is not confined to Christians: the struggle is Everyman's, since everyone is a son before becoming a father. Does one have to cease being a son before one can become a father? Does one have to deny, kill one's father (the Oedipus complex) before one can cease being a child? Psychologists will tell you of the difficulties and conflicts that arise from father-fixation, and religious educationalists would do well to listen to them, instead of believing that there is a "ready-made" solution.

What are the conditions for becoming an adult while still keeping affection and respect for one's father?

First—one becomes adult vis-à-vis one's father when one no longer expects anything from him.

"What? Are you suggesting we should no longer expect anything from God?"

Yes, that would be an adult attitude: not to hanker after

presents, not to "count" on other people, to recognize that *what we ask of God, God can only do through us.*

Second—when one knows that he has already given us everything.

A true father has given his son freedom. A true father keeps back nothing that will make his son remain subject to him. He has given him so much that he sends him out before him, to become a father in his turn.

Dependence always engenders irritation, worry, and aggression. One can only love truly in freedom. Think of your physical parents: your relationship with them becomes easy once they have given you enough to free yourself from them. Then you can turn back to them with joy and gratitude, can usefully ask their advice, and can come to see, day by day, how much they have given you by realizing how much you are capable of.

God sets us free. This is what is meant by believing that God is our Father.

So a prayer that is both truly adult and truly filial would have two "movements":

The first—thanksgiving: an affirmation of joy, pride and confidence in the recognition of all that we have received: "All that is yours is mine."

Christian prayer is a continual inventory, a cataloguing of the wonders God has done for us, a recognition, a taking stock and giving thanks. There is no end to our realization of how privileged we are, no end to our penetration with the tenderness and generosity of the Father, no end to the confidence we can gain in him so as to be forced to gain confidence in ourselves.

The second—commitment: when one has been given everything, there is nothing left except giving in one's turn. A father gives the gift of fatherhood; God gives the gift of Godhood to others, of doing for others what he has done for us.

This is why the structure of the prayer I am suggesting

will always consist of two movements: I regard the "Our Father" as having a first movement of calling to mind God's plan, and a second movement of man's commitment to it.

WHO ART IN HEAVEN.

What an awful way to start! As soon as you tell a child that, it puts him off. We may be blasé enough not to find any difficulty in it, but a fresh mind, one that still thinks about what it says, is immediately alienated. To tell someone today that God is in his heaven is to make him leave God out of account on earth. "Our Father, who art in heaven . . . stay there!", as Prévert mocks. It means that God has shut himself away, planted himself up in heaven, away from all this down below, thought better of the human exercise, got tired of man—and so is no longer of any interest to man.

Our imagery is so decayed that Gagarin's naïve remark, which theologians affect to scoff at: "I didn't find God up there," in fact finds a spontaneous echo in the mind of every child of today. Try telling a young boy who has lost his father: "Your Daddy's in heaven."

"Who art in heaven" is not only meaningless: it is the exact opposite of what Christ was trying to tell us. For the Semitic mind, the setting of God in heaven was the means of making him seem close to us; nowadays it expresses his distance from us. For them, he had to occupy an exalted position if he was to concern himself with mankind; if he had been on earth, he could only have bothered with those immediately surrounding him. He would not have been able to see the wood for the trees. He had to be in a dominant position to keep his eye on us; he had to be in heaven in order to be on earth!

But for us today, a spiritual presence has to be outside time and space. I am infinitely more present to those I am thinking about and love than to those who elbow and shove me in the subway. For us, God can be with each of us without our having to look up to him in heaven.

So the translation should be: "Our Father, you are with us." The amendment is of capital importance, whatever the theologians may think. They, and perhaps you too, are intelligent enough to read the right meaning into each formula and make the necessary amendments as they go. But if you say one thing and think another, why not tell your children what you think directly, since they still believe that words are supposed to mean what they say, and signs to signify what they mean?

We have come to the stage where the sacraments, which are supposed to be tangible signs, are so lacking in meaning and so intangible that they need commentary, explanation, historical examination. And with every word in the "religious" vocabulary, one has to stop and think that it probably does not mean what it usually means, but has some special meaning, quite different.

When will we learn to say things straight, when will we learn to put words, sacraments, traditions of every age, the Church itself, at the service of man, not man at the service of all these things?

Is it a small thing to proclaim (or deny) that the only dwelling place of God is man, that there is no heaven, no other world, no future life but only an eternal life which begins as soon as we know the one true God and Jesus Christ whom he has sent (John 17, 3)? God came into this world and did not leave it. He is with us forever. He does not live either in heaven or in churches, as badly instructed children think: he has established his dwelling among us.

Is it a small thing to tell children whose father has died that their father is in heaven, happy with God, while they are left orphans? Or to tell them the good news that Christ did not want us to think of ourselves as "orphans," left desolate; that he has come back to us, that though the world may see him no more, we can see him because he lives in us and so we live too (John 14, 18–19)? And that their father has no more abandoned them than Jesus has; that their father is with Christ, that he always lives to make intercession for them (Hebrews 7, 25), and that they can find him again in each of their communions, because by communing with Christ we are united to all those who live his life?

Then come three phrases of which it has not been said often enough that they are not requests, but wishes. But who will grant these wishes: God or you? The whole question is here. Is your faith one of waiting and sighing, or is it a commitment that makes you responsible for carrying out God's plan? In other words, who is at fault, who is letting the other down: God or you?

HALLOWED BE THY NAME

Do you dare ask God to make his name holy? Do you think he has not already done so, or that he will do so better because you ask him to?

God has made holy. He has revealed his name, which is his love. No one can do better and God will never go beyond this. The Father is naked on the cross: "Who sees me, sees the Father." Who taught the Son to love like that? The Father! "The Father who is in me works in me." Only the Son listened to the Father enough to say this so faithfully.

Before his passion, Christ said: "Now the Son of man has been glorified, and God has been glorified in him." It is on the cross that God reveals his name, makes it holy, hallows it. If you wait for a new or a better revelation of God's love, you are going back to Old Testament times, still waiting for a glorious Messiah.

No, there is only one thing left to do: complete the revelation of this love, spread the Good News. We will make his love known as fathers, mothers, brothers, and sisters. The way we love will show others the Father who taught us, will show them who our Father is.

THY KINGDOM COME

If you are waiting for the kingdom of God to come, you will have a long wait: it has come, it is "in the midst of you" (Luke 17, 20–21).

There are Christians who dare to laugh at the Jews for still waiting for the Messiah. After the capture of Jerusalem in the Six-Day War, one newspaper said: "The Jews are weeping for joy at the Wailing Wall." But do Christians look any happier in their "vale of tears"?

The kingdom is in the midst of us. Who can make it grow? God? If so, then he is badly at fault. Luckily he has your prayers to make him do better, to recall him to his duties! No, God has set up his tent in the midst of us, but like the smallest of all the seeds that will nevertheless grow into a great tree capable of sheltering the birds of the air. How will it grow? I know, and you know: through you, by your efforts, obviously!

We must surely democratize religious language, abandon the imperialistic, regal vocabulary we use: "deign," "supreme majesty," "throne"—even the Blessed Virgin is called "august"! You'll see, in three hundred years they will have progressed as far as calling Christ "President"—when there will be no more republics to be president of.

But Christ said: "I do not call you servants, but friends." All right, we have a biblical heritage, agreed, and we cannot escape from it, but on top of it we have piled a heritage of Platonism, Aristotelianism, Roman imperialism, feudalism, and monarchism. And modern man is suffocating under the weight of all these, like David in Saul's armor.

So let us say: "You have set up your house among us, you have made man your real dwelling place, and we want to show every man his dignity as your home, to show respect to it and to make everyone respect it."

THY WILL BE DONE ON EARTH AS IT IS IN HEAVEN

In Christ, God has fulfilled his purpose of love: he has

healed the sick, reconciled sinners, rehabilitated strangers and pagans, raised the dead to life, given us his peace and his joy, and united all the scattered children of God in one Body.

Now it is our turn to take over this immense task of relieving the poverty and hunger in the world. It is up to us to realize our responsibility and exercise our power of forgiveness, of healing, of transfiguration, of multiplication of loaves, of resurrection and peace!

GIVE US THIS DAY OUR DAILY BREAD

Here, unfortunately, we are starting to demand things, and as it stands this is the most dangerous formula in the prayer.

In Christ's time, it was not so. Then people believed that everything came direct from God; they had no concept of natural laws and secondary causes, but attributed everything in man and in nature to God. It was God who destroyed Sodom and Gomorrah in a volcanic eruption, God who hardened Pharaoh's heart so that he did not listen to Moses, and if the Hebrews wiped out whole tribes, massacring the women and children, it was clearly the will of God that they should do so.

Not that they were more stupid than we are; they knew the meaning of words. They knew that to ask God for bread was not to dispense men from working to produce it. But their means of production were so puny compared to the forces of nature that they modestly overlooked their part in the sequence and attributed the results directly to the prime cause, God.

Two things have changed: modern man no longer worships nature; he has mastered it and can therefore only believe in God by distinguishing him carefully from nature. And the balance between nature and men's means of production has completely changed, so that men now are insulted by any insinuation that they are parasites of nature and beggars before God. Modern atheism is the rediscovery of human dignity and the creative calling of man. And both these concepts are essentially Christian. So why have men of good faith only rediscovered them and felt able to affirm them by rejecting the Church? And the Church has done nothing to put them right, since it spontaneously and continually regards these notions as inimical to it. Where do the dignity and creativity of man come into the "Our Father" as we teach it to our children?

What is one to think of a God whose joy consists in having people ask him for things all the time, who makes not only his children's supply of bread, but their whole well-being depend on his whim, who keeps his children permanently in the position of guilty beggars?

Yes, in a way everything comes from God, but God's real gift to man is the independence that allows him to be a creator in his turn. And modern man has a sharp and even touchy appreciation of this point.

Imagine a mother exclaiming ecstatically to her daughter today: "God is giving us another baby!" What would the reaction be? "Mommy, do you still think I believe in all that stuff?" And surely our modern girl is totally right in standing up for the autonomy of secondary causes? If she knows the details of the facts of conception, and quite probably those of contraception as well, what's the use of trying to make her believe that childbirth depends on divine providence?

Such an attempt could only be conducive to atheism, and for two reasons: it attacks the dignity of man and strips him of respect for his work. It was, I think, Père Michonneau who said that the reason the working class lost the faith in the nineteenth century was not so much the Church's anti-social attitude as the fact that its explanation of the origins of the world in terms of Genesis was contradictory to the recent discoveries of science. And it is also true that if God is the one who gives bread, then he is the one who takes it away, and in a world where two out of every three people go hungry, that is a sure way to atheism.

Once again, I am sure that when you say: "give us this day our daily bread," you are intelligent enough not to believe that the result will be a shower of loaves on the Indians or the Chinese. God has only one way of giving the Indians enough to eat: in the short term, by our producing more bread and sharing it out; in the long term, by our educating them to become self-sufficient, through paying reasonable prices for their produce, through long-term loans at low-interest rates, and by a sensible population policy.

But why don't you tell your children this? Why put their backs up with phrases that mean nothing to them, that will turn them into atheists as soon as they think about what you are making them say? (And they will think better and quicker than you.) If they are hungry (or sorry for those who are), they will be indignant about what this God does not grant; if they work, they will smile at your prayer just like children who have found out who Santa Claus really is.

But the effect could be even worse: there is a danger that they will believe you, that they will go off and pray piously for God to multiply loaves, that they will slot themselves into the level of mystification and alienation at which God dispenses us from being men. Have you never met anyone so stupefied, drugged by piety as to have reached this point?

"And give bread to those who have none!" Have you ever heard a crueller, more cynical prayer? And this is the daily prayer of countless Christian families. That is the way to share our labors: we sit down to table and God looks after the rest! How reassuring of him! It leaves me with a clear conscience as well as a full stomach. No depression in sight, not even in the billfold!

No, say rather: "You have shared your bread with us, and I know what it cost you. Bread supports life; he who gives his bread, gives his life. By sharing your bread with me, you have given me your life, you have shown me how much you

love me." Greater love than this has no man, than to lay
down his life . . . "I feed myself on your bread and your
life so as to wake up to love, live and share like you!"

There is an extra problem in this bit: we seem to be setting God a good example—we forgive, so you forgive. Obviously the reverse is true and if informed Christians can
understand the formula aright (it's a question of degree,
not of cause: we will be forgiven to the extent that we forgive our brothers), they should tell beginners: "It means,
'You have forgiven us to such an extent that you have shown
us the degree of tact, respect and joy with which we should
be reconciled to our brothers'."

The formula is justifiable, but not in the way most people
think. It is like the ending of the parable of the wicked servant (Matthew 18, 34): "And in anger his lord delivered
him to the jailers . . ." Do you think God acts in anger,
punishes, avenges himself? If you do, your thinking is still
at the mythological stage.

God punishes no one; God is love. But man punishes himself; man deprives himself of what he needs most in the
world—loving and being loved. This is why God's judgment
is never an "execution" but simply a confrontation: God is
forced to recognize that his forgiveness and love have not
taught this servant to love and forgive. God's forgiveness
has not "bitten," or, as one says of a vaccination, "taken." If
he does not know how to forgive, it is because forgiveness
has not got through to him.

Do not think that the lord is avenging himself by taking
back the forgiveness he has already given; no, he can only
go on the evidence: since this man is manifestly incapable
of passing on forgiveness, he cannot be open to being forgiven. This is just the opposite of what Christ said of Mary

Magdalen: "Much will be forgiven her because she has loved much."

But one can wonder if this is the way most people are led to think by this formula in the "Our Father." They are more likely to imagine that they merit God's forgiveness, whereas in fact it is God who longs to forgive them infinitely more than they wish to be forgiven.

Do not constantly make yourself out better than the God you pray to: that way lies atheism!

AND LEAD US NOT INTO TEMPTATION

This really is the end! It seems that since a formula has to be retained that will satisfy Orthodox, Protestants, and Catholics, this translation is with us for a bit yet. But it is all very well to try for unity of expression around the world when there is a gap of two thousand years between the first use of the phrase and its use today: those two thousand years have completely changed the meaning.

Literalism of this sort is actually infidelity to the original; it is respecting words instead of meaning. Besides, if revelation is indeed "news," surely it has to be handed on in terms that will sound to each generation as though they are hearing it for the first time. And if it is "good news," how can it be handed on by insinuating that God can lead us into temptation? Listening to some professional purveyors of the so-called message, one is more likely to regard it as bad and old than good and new.

God does not lead anyone. God proposes and man disposes; God does not dispose of us. We live under a rule of grace, not one of power. Read the Gospels: Christ proposes, not imposes: "If you wish . . ." God is a beggar, standing at the door, knocking . . .

And God does not tempt: "Let no one say when he is tempted, 'I am tempted by God'; for God cannot be tempted with evil, and he himself tempts no one" (James 1, 13).

Those who defend the formula as it stands will say that if one attacks it one is showing ignorance of the biblical sense of the word "temptation," which does not have the pejorative meaning we attach to it, but means simply "test," a test sent by God so that we can show what is in our heart. But does this really make it any better? Either it is something bad, so how can we suppose that God will lead us into it? Or it is something good, so why do we ask God not to lead us into it?

Christian Duquoc writes: "The Church and the Christian pray daily for God to emerge from his silence, to shorten the time he leaves us without the protection of his benevolent power," and, "The Christian asks God not to be put to the test, which means not to be left by God in a situation that does not witness to God's love." So, a situation in which God fails to reveal himself, in which God is not love, so in which God is not God! What a strange God: try not to be like him!

No, it seems too difficult to extract any real meaning from the present formula. I would rather say: "You are with us in all our trials; you are nailed to all our crosses; you die in all our deaths. And your gift to us is to suffer and die in love and faith."

BUT DELIVER US FROM EVIL

God has delivered us from evil by revealing to us that it is always right to love, that love conquers evil and can, even from the cross, convert those who crucify you. Now it is your turn to deliver others. Say, then: "You showed us how to set captives free, as you freed Mary Magdalen from the ties of the flesh, Zaccheus from money, and Matthew from his depressing job. And this love of yours brought them happiness and freedom. So with you, through you and in you, I will free the world from evil."

Is this not the essence of the Gospel message, the essence that we must lead men today to find in their daily prayer, in the first prayer they learn? Modern men and women will say the "Our Father" with pride and joy when they are able to say it in a spirit that is both filial and adult, as grateful and yet responsible beings, when they can all say it together as a thanksgiving and a program of action: "Father, I know you always listen to me; Father, all that is yours is mine. Father, you have given me so much that you have given me more than the gift of receiving: you have given me the gift of giving. I have nothing more to ask than time to let your gifts sink into me. And when I am filled with you, I shall have given myself entirely to others."

Christ is just as much the revelation of man as the revelation of God. Being so truly God made him the only true man who has ever lived. This is why, formed by him, taught and nourished by him, we take heart and say:

"Our Father, you are with us,

"You have shown and taught us your love, and we shall live in it so that we can pass it on to all those who wait for it, through our friendships, our brotherhood, our parenthood;

"You have come to live in us, and we want to show every man his dignity, and win for him the respect he deserves;

"In Jesus Christ you have made known your wish for justice, for sharing and loving, and we want to carry out your wish on this earth so that it will become a place where justice reigns and all men love their fellow men;

"You have shared your bread with us so well that you have made us capable of sharing ours as well;

"You have forgiven us so well that you have taught us the tact, respect, and joy with which we must make friends again with our brothers;

"You are with us in all our trials, in all our temptations

and sufferings, to give us strength to overcome them lik
you;

"And with you, in you and through you, we will free th
world from evil."

"Amen!"

OTHER IMAGE BOOKS

These prices subject to change without notice

OTHER IMAGE BOOKS

A WOMAN CLOTHED WITH THE SUN – Edited by John J. Delaney (D118) – $1.45

INTERIOR CASTLE – St. Teresa of Avila (Translated by E. Allison Peers) – (D120) – $1.45

THE GREATEST STORY EVER TOLD – Fulton Oursler (D121) – $1.45

LIVING FLAME OF LOVE – St. John of the Cross (Translated by E. Allison Peers) – (D129) – $1.45

A HISTORY OF PHILOSOPHY: VOLUME 1 – GREECE AND ROME (2 Parts) – Frederick Copleston, S.J. (D134a, D134b) – $1.75 ea.

A HISTORY OF PHILOSOPHY: VOLUME 2 – MEDIAEVAL PHILOSOPHY (2 Parts) – Frederick Copleston, S.J. Part I – Augustine to Bonaventure. Part II – Albert the Great to Duns Scotus (D135a, D135b) – $1.75 ea.

A HISTORY OF PHILOSOPHY: VOLUME 3 – LATE MEDIAEVAL AND RENAISSANCE PHILOSOPHY (2 Parts) – Frederick Copleston, S.J. Part I – Ockham to the Speculative Mystics. Part II – The Revival of Platonism to Suárez (D136a, D136b) – $1.45 ea.

A HISTORY OF PHILOSOPHY: VOLUME 4 – MODERN PHILOSOPHY: Descartes to Leibniz – Frederick Copleston, S.J. (D137) – $1.75

A HISTORY OF PHILOSOPHY: VOLUME 5 – MODERN PHILOSOPHY: The British Philosophers, Hobbes to Hume (2 Parts) – Frederick Copleston, S.J. Part I – Hobbes to Paley (D138a) – $1.45. Part II – Berkeley to Hume (D138b) – $1.75

A HISTORY OF PHILOSOPHY: VOLUME 6 – MODERN PHILOSOPHY (2 Parts) – Frederick Copleston, S.J. Part I – The French Enlightenment to Kant (D139a) – $1.45; (D139b) – $1.75

A HISTORY OF PHILOSOPHY: VOLUME 7 – MODERN PHILOSOPHY (2 Parts) – Frederick Copleston, S.J. Part I – Fichte to Hegel. Part II – Schopenhauer to Nietzsche (D140a, D140b) – $1.75 ea.

A HISTORY OF PHILOSOPHY: VOLUME 8 – MODERN PHILOSOPHY: Bentham to Russell (2 Parts) – Frederick Copleston, S.J. Part I – British Empiricism and the Idealist Movement in Great Britain. Part II – Idealism in America, the Pragmatist Movement, the Revolt against Idealism (D141a, D141b) – $1.45 ea.

A DOCTOR AT CALVARY – Pierre Barbet, M.D. A moving account of the Passion of our Lord (D155) – 95¢

These prices subject to change without notice

OTHER IMAGE BOOKS

THE SPIRITUAL EXERCISES OF ST. IGNATIUS – Translated by Anthony Mottola, Ph.D. Introduction by Robert W. Gleason, S.J. (D170) – $1.25

THE WAY OF PERFECTION – St. Teresa of Avila. Trans. and ed. by E. Allison Peers (D176) – $1.45

LIFE AND HOLINESS – Thomas Merton. Exposition of the principles of the spiritual life (D183) – 85¢

MY LIFE WITH CHRIST – Anthony J. Paone, S.J. (D185) – $1.45

A FAMILY ON WHEELS: Further Adventures of the Trapp Family Singers – Maria Augusta Trapp with Ruth T. Murdoch (D187) – $1.25

WITH GOD IN RUSSIA – Walter J. Ciszek, S.J., with Daniel L. Flaherty, S.J. (D200) – $1.45

THE TWO-EDGED SWORD – John L. McKenzie, S.J. Outstanding interpretation of the Old Testament (D215) – $1.45

THE LILIES OF THE FIELD – William E. Barrett (D225) – $1.25

NO MAN IS AN ISLAND – Thomas Merton (D231) – $1.45

AND YOUNG MEN SHALL SEE VISIONS – Andrew M. Greeley. Letters to a young collegian on subjects of burning interest to young men today (D232) – 85¢

CONJECTURES OF A GUILTY BYSTANDER – Thomas Merton. A collection of notes, opinions, reflections (D234) – $1.75

THE POWER OF LOVE – Fulton J. Sheen (D235) – $1.25

THE STORY OF THOMAS MORE – John Farrow (D236) – 95¢

THE NOONDAY DEVIL: Spiritual Support in Middle Age – Bernard Basset, S.J. A funny-serious book of spiritual direction (D237) – $1.25

HEALTH OF MIND AND SOUL – Ignace Lepp (D239) – 95¢

RELIGION AND PERSONALITY – Adrian van Kaam, C.S.Sp. (D240) – $1.45

RELIGIONS OF THE WORLD (2 Volumes) – John A. Hardon, S.J. An account of the history, beliefs, and practices of the major religions of the world (D241a) – $1.75; (D241b) – $1.45

MOMENTS OF TRUTH – Edited by Dan Herr and Joel Wells. An anthology portraying crises of the human spirit by 16 great authors (D243) – 95¢

CHRISTIAN SACRAMENTS AND CHRISTIAN PERSONALITY – Bernard J. Cooke, S.J. (D246) – $1.25

THOUGHTS IN SOLITUDE – Thomas Merton (D247) – 95¢

These prices subject to change without notice

OTHER IMAGE BOOKS

These prices subject to change without notice

OTHER IMAGE BOOKS

These prices subject to change without notice

OTHER IMAGE BOOKS

CHRISTIANITY IN THE TWENTIETH CENTURY – John A. Hardon (D310) – $2.45

THE OLD TESTAMENT OF THE JERUSALEM BIBLE – Reader's Edition – Alexander Jones, General Editor
Volume 1: Genesis – Ruth (D311) – $1.95
Volume 2: 1 Samuel – 2 Maccabees (D312) – $1.95
Volume 3: Job – Ecclesiasticus (D313) – $1.95
Volume 4: The Prophets – Malachi (D314) – $1.95

CHRISTIAN COMMUNITY: Response to Reality – Bernard J. Cooke (D315) – $1.45

THE JESUS MYTH – Andrew M. Greeley (D316) – $1.25

THE SURVIVAL OF DOGMA – Avery Dulles, S.J. (D317) – $1.45

LIVING IN HOPE – Ladislaus Boros, S.J. (D318) – $1.25

LOVE IS ALL – Joseph and Lois Bird (D319) – $1.25

THE SOUL AFIRE: Revelations of the Mystics – Ed. by H. A. Reinhold (D320) – $1.95

CONTEMPLATION IN A WORLD OF ACTION – Thomas Merton (D321) – $1.95

AN AUGUSTINE READER (An Image Original) – Edited with an Intro. by John J. O'Meara (D322) – $2.45

HOPE IS THE REMEDY – Bernard Häring, C.Ss.R. (D323) – $1.25

SEX: THOUGHTS FOR CONTEMPORARY CHRISTIANS – Edited by Michael J. Taylor, S.J. (D324) – $1.45

THE CLOUD OF UNKNOWING (and THE BOOK OF PRIVY COUNSELING) – Newly edited with an Intro. by William Johnston, S.J. (D325) – $1.45

WE ARE FUTURE – Ladislaus Boros, S.J. (D326) – $1.45

LET'S START PRAYING AGAIN – Bernard Basset, S.J. (D327) – $1.25

THE NEW SEXUALITY: Myths, Fables and Hang-ups – Eugene C. Kennedy (D328) – $1.45

THE PAIN OF BEING HUMAN – Eugene C. Kennedy (D329) – $1.75

POWER TO THE PARENTS! – Joseph and Lois Bird (D330) – $1.45

A HARSH AND DREADFUL LOVE – William D. Miller (D331) – $1.95

CATHOLIC AMERICA – John Cogley (D332) – $1.45

TO LIVE IS TO LOVE – Ernesto Cardenal (D333) – $1.45

PROTESTANTISM – Martin E. Marty (D334) – $2.45

THE SUPPER OF THE LAMB – Robert Farrar Capon (D335) – $1.75

These prices subject to change without notice

A 74–6

Heat   1500.
Rent   700
Electric   300
Gas   50
Trash   15¢
Water
food   1300
          _____
           3865

15 singles @ 250. = 3750

Committment – Involvement

Building up the Body
1 Cor 12 - vs 12 - Bodies have many
Parts – Each part necessary.

Priest became everything
    people expected... from priest
People didn't think – let priest do
Prophesy..."will you be willing
    to work for this cause?"

Acts 8
Every Christian was a witness
to Christ!
Why did the apostles have such
power to convert? Pentecost!
Only reason to be filled w
the Spirit is to Bear Witness
to Jesus. to Build up the Body
1st to cleanse your body –